Screen-Free CRAFTS KIDS WILL LOVE

HANDS-ON PROJECTS THAT PROMOTE LEARNING

LYNN LILLY and the {CraftBoxGirls} Team

Ulysses Press

Published in the U.S. by
Ulysses Press
P.O. Box 3440
Berkeley, CA 94703
www.ulyssespress.com

ISBN: 978-1-61243-564-0
Library of Congress Control Number 2015952138

Printed in the United States by Bang Printing

10 9 8 7 6 5 4 3 2 1

Acquisitions editor: Casie Vogel
Project editor: Bridget Thoreson
Managing editor: Claire Chun
Editor: Renee Rutledge
Proofreader: Melanie Field
Front cover design: Michelle Thompson
Interior design: Jake Flaherty

Distributed by Publishers Group West

IMPORTANT NOTE TO READERS: This book is independently authored and published and no sponsorship or endorsement of this book by, and no affiliation with, any trademarked brands or other products mentioned or pictured within is claimed or suggested. All trademarks that appear in materials/ingredients lists, photographs, and elsewhere in this book belong to their respective owners and are used here for informational purposes only. The authors and publishers encourage readers to patronize the quality brands mentioned and pictured in this book.

CONTENTS

INTRODUCTION

Crafting is an art, a passion and an expression that brings joy to all ages. Our team wrote this book to inspire and enliven children and families through creativity. In the day and age of computers, phones, tablets and many digital devices, we wanted to create a book that would bring children back to the roots of playing and having fun without technology. These projects are designed to get children away from the screen and encourage them to explore their creativity, follow instructions and cultivate important skills.

The projects and activities in this book are for everyone. We included recommended minimum ages for each project as a guideline for the difficulty level. An adult should supervise at least the beginning phases of every project, no matter how old the child. We know crafting books can sometimes be overwhelming, so we created a recommended supply list to get you and your child started on your creative journey. We also recommend our favorite sources for shopping tips.

Where to get started? The fun part about a crafting book is that you don't have to start at the beginning. Does your child love play dates with friends or have a slumber party coming up? If so, we recommend starting with the Party Time chapter, which is filled with fun ideas for friends, groups and parties. Are you looking for craft projects that will entertain your children after they make them? Start with the Toys and Games chapter for great projects that will entertain your children long after they finish making them. Does your child love the kitchen and want to be a future chef? Introduce them to the In the Kitchen chapter that features easy recipes you and your child can make together, as well as crafts using ingredients found in the kitchen. No matter where you start, this book is filled with fun and exciting projects that your child will love to make and be proud to display! Don't let your child have all the fun, jump in and craft with them. The projects in this book are great for the whole family to help with and enjoy together.

We would love to see your child's finished projects. Please share them with us on Twitter or Instagram by using #cbgkids and tagging @craftboxgirls.

Happy creating!

To the Kids

We created this book for you! We hope you are inspired to create amazing things. Use this book to jump-start your creative path. Take the skills you learn to create your own projects, teach your friends and share with others.

Creativity is a gift that you should embrace! Always remember to dream big, live life to the fullest, chase what seems impossible and, most importantly, love yourself because you are GREAT!

Recommended Supplies and Resources

We always recommend having a stash of standard craft supplies and tools. You will see these materials show up in many of the projects in this book.

- Foam brushes
- Mod Podge
- Paintbrushes
- Acrylic paint
- Ruler
- Scissors
- Construction paper
- Parchment paper
- Double-sided tape
- Clear tape
- School glue
- Fabric glue
- Pencils
- Permanent markers
- Hot glue gun and glue sticks
- Washi/decorative tape
- Alphabet stickers

Shopping Tips

We buy an absurd amount of craft supplies and are always looking for the best deal and quality products. Always check retailer websites and applications for coupons. Sign up for store email lists because the big-box retailers often send out exclusive coupons and sales to their email subscribers.

Our top shopping destinations:

- www.michaels.com
- www.amazon.com
- www.plaidonline.com
- www.save-on-crafts.com
- www.factorydirectcraft.com

PROJECT GALLERY

Toys and Games

Kids have lots of free time, which means you need a lot of toys and games to keep them out of trouble. This chapter is filled with ideas for toys kids can make on their own to keep them busy playing games long after the craft is complete. These projects are great for kids to make and play with together to boost social skills. Happy playtime!

Chore Track, p. 10

Homemade Kite, p. 12

Liquid Sidewalk Chalk, p. 15

Friendship Bracelet, p. 16

Never-Ending Tic-Tac-Toe, p. 18

Foosball Box Game, p. 20

Shoebox Oven, p. 22

Duct Tape Shield & Sword, p. 24

Superhero Cape & Cuffs, p. 26

Robot Box Head, p. 28

Party Time

Every day is a day to celebrate! The Party Time chapter is filled with fun and colorful projects, party inspiration, sleepover fun, and play date ideas for your kids to share with their friends. These ideas will keep the kiddos busy all day or night long and keep your stress level low. Party on!

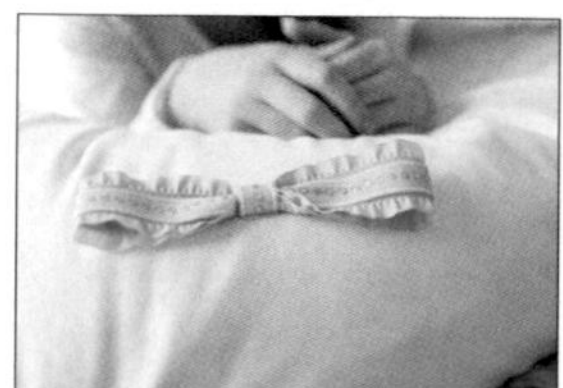

Pillowcase Decoration, p. 30

Fleece Blanket, p. 32

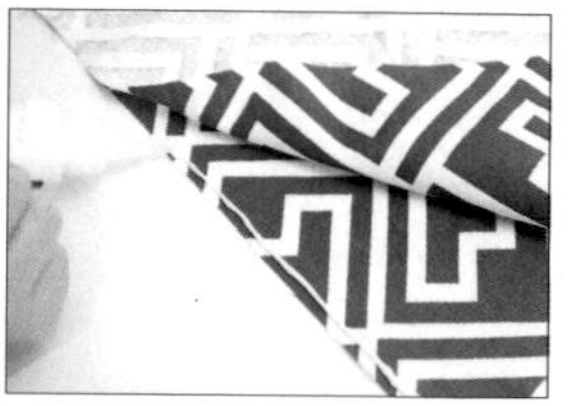

No-Sew Playtime Pillow, p. 34

Homemade Sleepover Tent, p. 36

Ribbon Dancer Wand, p. 39

Flower Pen, p. 40

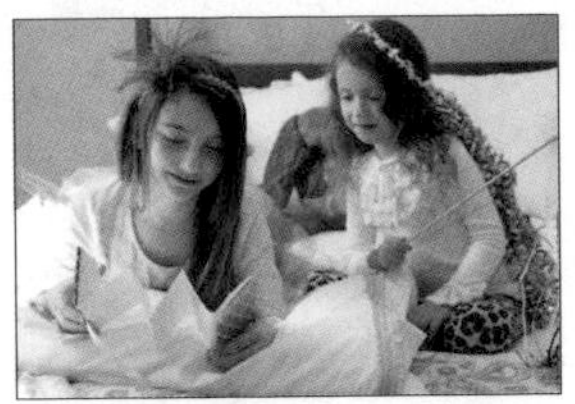

Accordion Notebook, p. 42

Homemade Headband, p. 45

Fishing Game, p. 46

Rain Stick, p. 49

Guitar, p. 50

Maracas, p. 53

Holidays

No matter what holidays you celebrate, these crafts are easy and fun, and can easily be modified to create crafts for any time of the year. For example, just switch up the color of paper for the July 4th Lanterns and you have a great year-round craft for the indoors or outdoors. Have a crafty holiday!

Valentine's Day Love Arrows, p. 54

Valentine's Day Garland, p. 56

S Patrick's Day Pencil Art, p. 57

Yarn Easter Eggs, p. 58

Chocolate Bunny Pops, p. 60

July 4th Lanterns, p. 62

Glow-in-the-Dark Spider Web, p. 64

Thankful Tree, p. 67

Salt Dough Ornament, p. 68

Art Decor

There is an artist inside every person. Help your child discover their creativity with these unique projects. This chapter will excite and inspire your child with new skills to become the artist they want to be.

Button Canvas Art, p. 70

Pizza Box Canvas Art, p. 72

Salt Art, p. 74

Watercolor Art: Salt and Crayon, p. 76

Painter's Tape Abstract Art, p. 79

Hand-Stamped Greeting Cards, p. 80

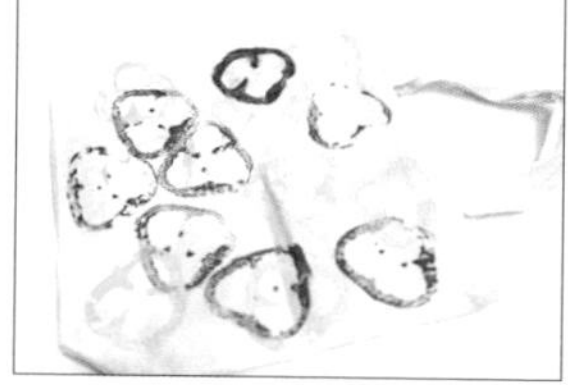

Vegetable-Stamped Tote Bag, p. 82

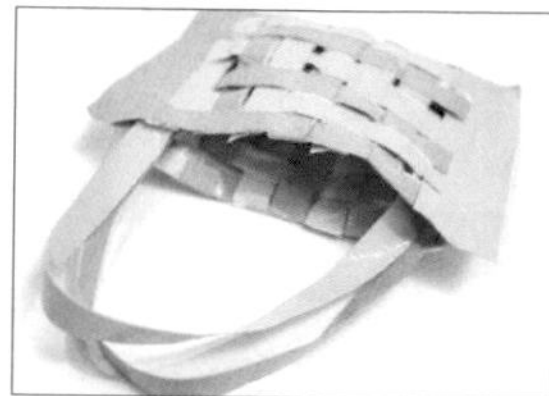

Duct Tape Tote Bag, p. 84

Terrarium, p. 86

Chalkboard Frame, p. 88

Tile Coasters, p. 90

Painted Bead Bracelet, p. 92

Dream Catcher, p. 94

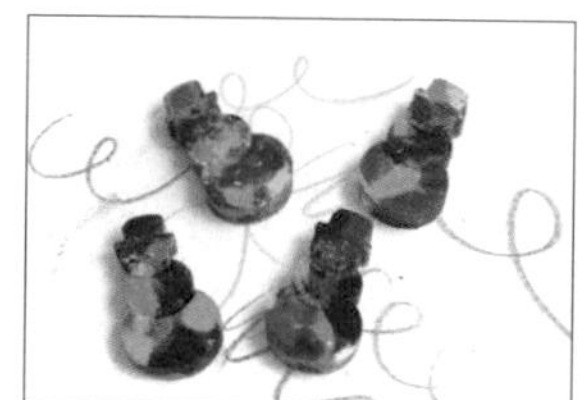

Recycled Crayon Molds, p. 95

In the Kitchen

The kitchen is the perfect place to challenge and teach your child everything from cooking to crafting. This chapter includes fun projects and easy recipes using simple ingredients to help introduce your child to kitchen tools and safety rules. Who knows, you might have a future star chef on your hands!

No-Sew Kitchen Apron, p. 96

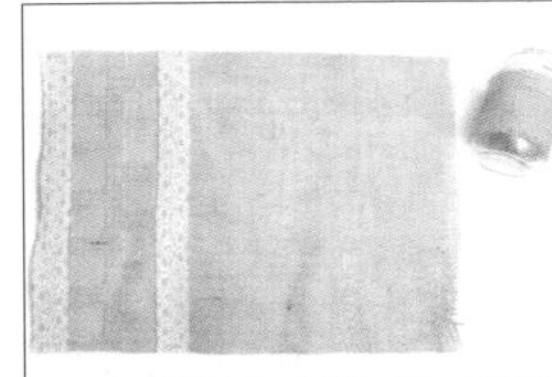
No-Sew Burlap Place Setting, p. 98

Recipe Book, p. 100

Chocolate Pretzel Popcorn, p. 102

Chocolate Bowls, p. 104

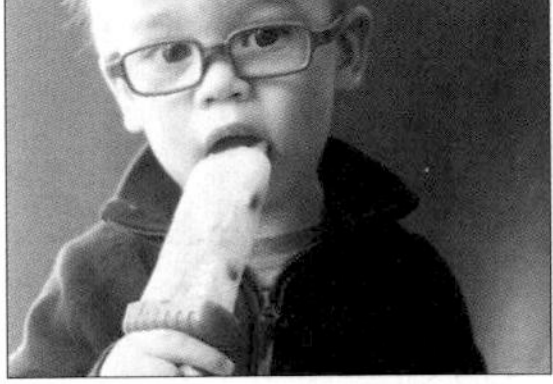
Organic Fruit Juice Candy Pops, p. 106

No-Bake Ice Cream Cake, p. 107

Two-Ingredient Fruit Roll-Ups, p. 109

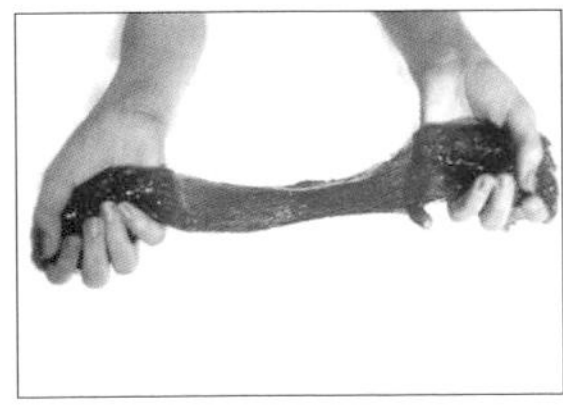
Goopy Goo, p. 110

Flavored Lip Balm, p. 112

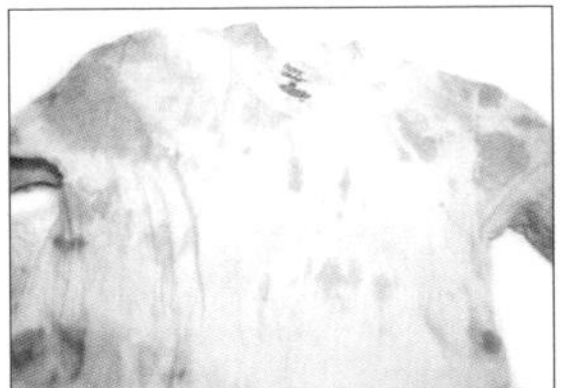
Food Color Tie-Dye Shirt, p. 113

Paper Lunch Bag Decorating, p. 115

Pets

Pets are just as much a part of the family as anyone else and are great friends for your children, so we've created a few easy crafts to make Fido's tail wag. We also included a bird feeder craft for those who don't have a household pet—bring beautiful birds to admire in your yard!

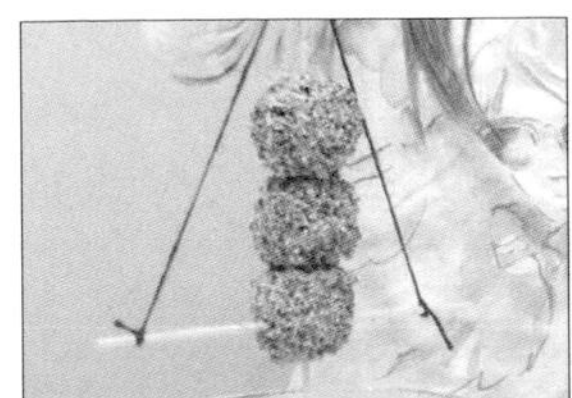
Bird Feeder, p. 118

Dog Collar Bow Tie, p. 120

Old T-Shirt Dog Toy, p. 123

Veggie Breath Dog Treats, p. 124

CHORE TRACK

Chores are normally boring and not the most fun thing to do in your free time. Why not turn your chores into a fun race game with this super-cool racetrack? Race to the finish line by customizing your chore board, and get your chores done before your parents have to remind you.

Age: 7+ with adult supervision

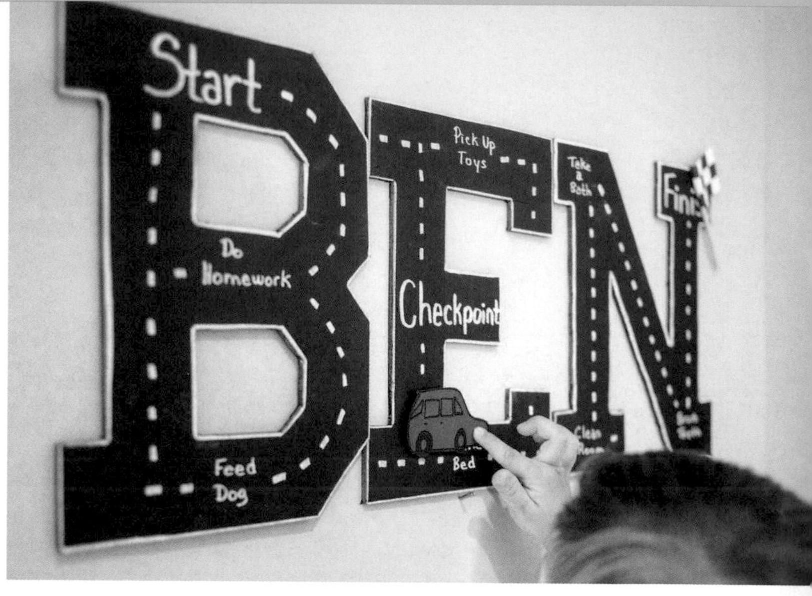

MATERIALS

- Black marker
- Red construction paper
- Scissors
- Checkered flag cardstock
- 1 thin dowel
- X-Acto knife
- School glue
- 1–2 black foam board(s)
- White chalk marker
- Masking tape

DIRECTIONS

1 Using the black marker, draw the outline of a car on the red construction paper.

2 Use the scissors to cut out the car along the lines you just drew.

3 Using the black marker, draw a rectangular flag on the checkered flag cardstock.

4 Cut out the flag with the scissors.

5 Have an adult help you cut 3 inches off the dowel using the X-Acto knife.

6 Roll the checkered flag around the 3 inch piece. Glue it in place. This is the finish line flag.

7 Use the black marker to draw your name in large block letters on the black foam board(s).

8 Have an adult use the X-Acto knife to cut out the letters on the foam board(s).

9 Use the white chalk marker to outline the letters.

10 Use the white chalk marker to label Start, Checkpoint and Finish on the first, middle, and last letters of your name. Tape the flag to the finish line.

11 Fill in your chores along the letters of your name using the white chalk marker.

12 Add dotted lines to make the racetrack lanes.

13 Tape the red car to the foam board to track your chores each day.

HOMEMADE KITE

Soar to new heights with this creative 3-D kite. This detailed project will challenge you to follow instructions and learn the art of building a 3-D structure. It is the perfect project for you to do with friends or siblings. Celebrate your accomplishment together by flying it high in the sky!

Age: 10+

MATERIALS

- 24 straws
- Scissors
- Roll of kitchen string
- 4 large sheets of tissue paper
- Pencil
- Clear tape

DIRECTIONS

1 Separate straws into four groups of six straws.

2 Form a triangle with three of the straws.

3 Measure and cut about 3 feet of string.

4 Thread the string through the straws, tying a knot to connect them as a triangle.

5 Add two more straws to continue to form a 3-D triangle, tying off knots at the ends to secure.

6 Add the remaining straw on the end of the string to complete the open side of the triangle. Tie a knot to secure the straw and leave 12 inches of excess string.

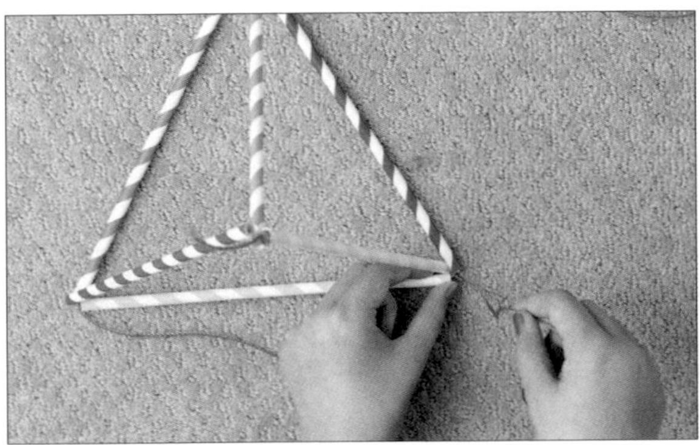

7 Repeat steps 2–6 three more times. You will have four 3-D triangles.

8 Lay a piece of tissue paper flat on your working surface. Place your first 3-D triangle on the tissue paper.

9 Trace one side of the triangle. Rotate over and trace the other side, forming a diamond shape.

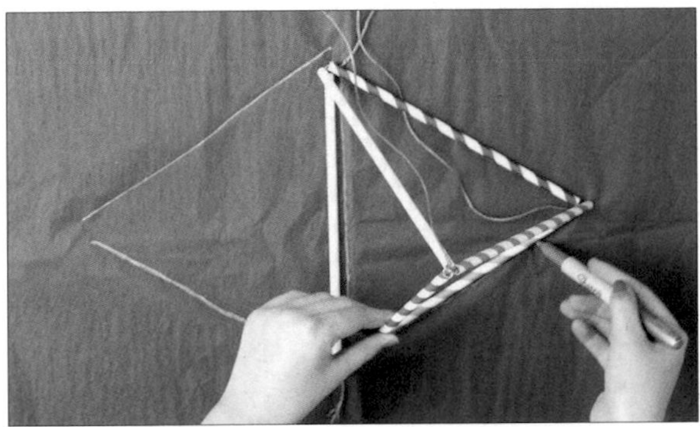

10 Draw flaps off the four outer sides of the diamond. Use the straws to measure the diamond.

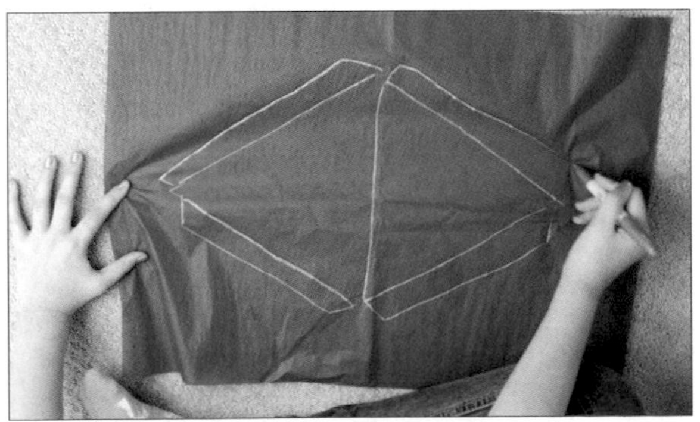

11 Cut out the diamond.

12 Once the diamond is cut out, lay the straw triangle back on the tissue paper.

13 Fold the flaps over the straws and secure with clear tape.

14 Complete steps 8–13 three more times for the remaining triangles.

15 Connect your triangles by tying the ends of the string together to form a pyramid of triangles.

16 Take the end of the string from the string roll and feed it through the outside straw on the open side of the top triangle. Take the excess string you left at each end of the straw and bring the ends together meeting at the center of the straw. Tie the ends together which will form a loose loop. Unravel when you are ready to use the kite.

17 You are now ready to fly your kite! Get a running start to watch your kite soar!

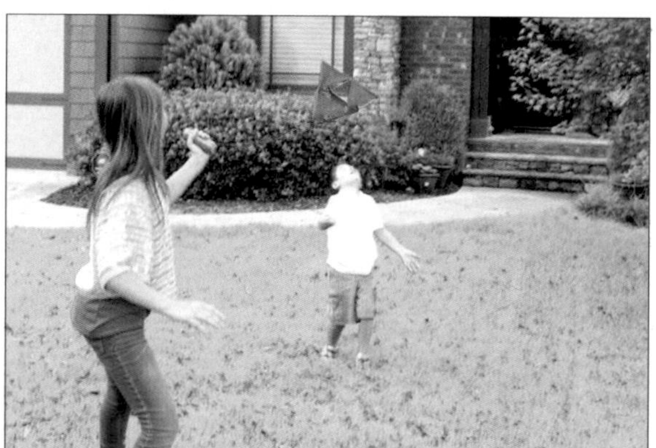

LIQUID SIDEWALK CHALK

Turn your driveway into a giant art project with homemade liquid sidewalk chalk. This easy recipe is made with everything your parents already have in the pantry. Create unique graffiti-style art with fun colors. Don't forget to grab a few friends to help make your driveway a work of art!

Age: 5+

MATERIALS

- 3 plastic condiment bottles at least 8 ounces
- 1 cup cornstarch
- 1 cup water
- 1 cup baking soda
- 3 colors of food coloring

DIRECTIONS

1 Open the lid of the first condiment bottle and pour in ⅓ cup cornstarch, ⅓ cup water, and ⅓ cup baking soda.

2 Add 7 drops of one color of food coloring.

3 Screw on the lid and put on the cap for the squeeze hole (if there is one). If not, put your finger over the squeeze hole.

4 Shake the bottle for 15–20 seconds to mix the ingredients. Check to see if completely mixed. If not, continue to shake until ingredients are well combined.

5 Repeat steps 1–4 for the other two bottles using a different color in each.

6 Take your bottles outside and start creating art by squirting the bottles. Write your name, draw a picture of your family or a day at the beach, or combine the colors for an artistic collage. The best part: this all washes off easily with water!

FRIENDSHIP BRACELET

Friends are forever and having a bracelet to show it makes it even better! Pick out string in you and your friend's favorite colors. We have two creative bracelet projects to showcase your friendship.

Age: 10+

MATERIALS

- Embroidery thread
- Scissors
- Beads (optional)

DIRECTIONS

Bracelet 1:

1 Cut three 48-inch-long pieces of embroidery thread.

2 Fold the strands together, tying them in the middle so there are six strands total. Tie a 1-inch loop 3 inches from the top.

3 Divide the embroidery strings into three separate, even groups.

4 Lay the right set of strings over and across the top of the center strings. Move the center strings to the right.

5 Lay the left set of strings over and across the top of the center strings. Move the center strings to the left.

6 Repeat.

7 After desired length is braided, tie a knot at the end. Leave 2–3 inches of string away from the knot and then cut off the excess.

8 Give it to your friend. Make a matching bracelet for yourself and rock your new style!

Bracelet 2:

1 Cut 3 strings of embroidery thread that are 48 inches long each.

2 Pull one string apart from the group.

3 Lay the string across the group leaving a space to the right of the main group. Loop the string around back and bring it through the hole.

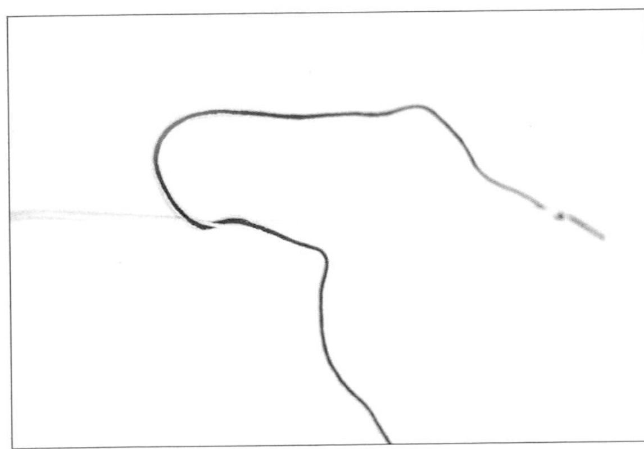

4 Repeat.

5 Add beads to a group of strings or an individual string for different effects.

6 After desired length is braided, tie a knot at the end. Leave 2–3 inches of string away from the knot and then cut off the excess. Repeat until desired length is braided, then tie knot at the end.

7 Glam it up with your BFF!

NEVER-ENDING TIC-TAC-TOE

Enjoy an endless game of tic-tac-toe with do-it-yourself stamps on a large piece of poster paper. You and your friends can play all day long. You can also take this game with you anywhere. Happy gaming!

Age: 9+ with adult supervision

MATERIALS

- (2) 1 x 1-inch cork squares
- Marker
- X-Acto knife
- Hot glue gun
- 2 wooden blocks
- 2 stamp pads
- White poster paper

DIRECTIONS

1 In block lettering, draw an "X" and an "O" on the cork with a marker.

2 Have an adult help you cut out the "X" and "O" using the X-Acto knife.

3 Using the hot glue gun, attach the "X" and "O" to the wooden blocks. Let them dry for five minutes.

4 Use the ink pads to stamp the "X" and "O" on the white poster paper for an endless game of tic-tac-toe.

FOOSBALL BOX GAME

Shoeboxes can make a ton of fun games. Save your next shoebox for this exciting game of foosball. Foosball will test your hand-eye coordination and give you quality social time with friends or your brothers and sisters.

Age: 8+

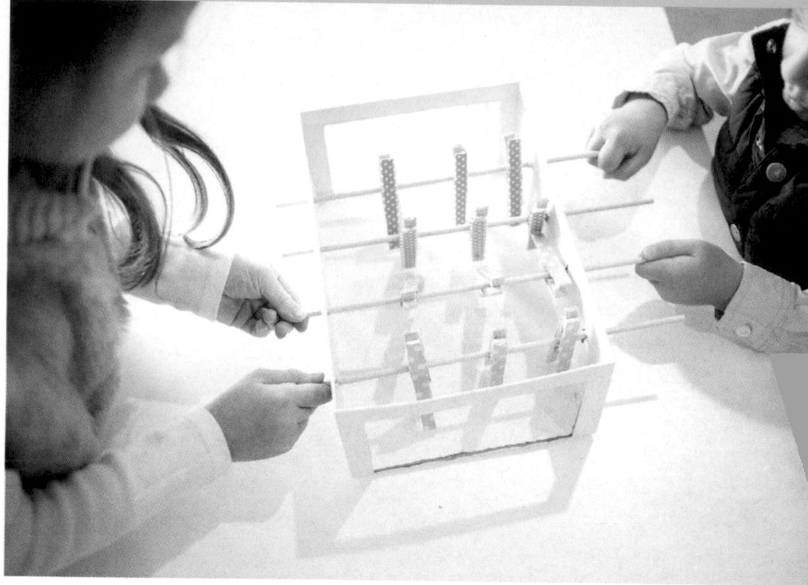

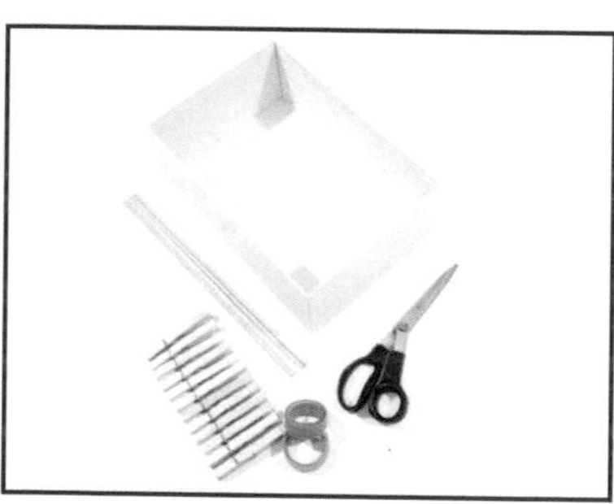

MATERIALS

- Shoebox
- Scissors
- 1 nail
- 4 thin dowels
- 2 different rolls of decorative or washi tape
- 12 clothespins

DIRECTIONS

1 On each end of the shoebox, cut out an opening for the goals.

2 Use the nail to poke four holes on each side of the shoebox. Poke the nail in the shoebox, rotate it to make the hole a little bigger, and remove and repeat for each of the four holes. Make sure the holes are evenly spaced out and midway from the top and bottom.

3 Insert the dowels to pierce from one hole to the hole on the other side of the shoebox. Do this with all four dowels.

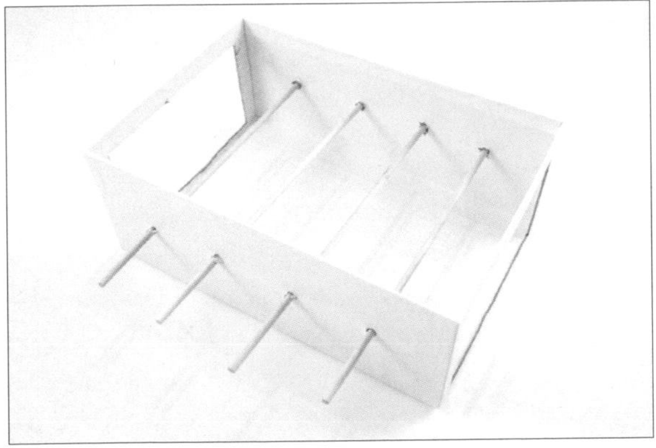

4 Apply washi tape to both sides of the clothespins. Six clothespins will be covered in one color washi tape and the other six will be covered in the alternate color. Each color represents a team.

5 Clip three matching-color clothespins to each dowel: three in the front and three in the back.

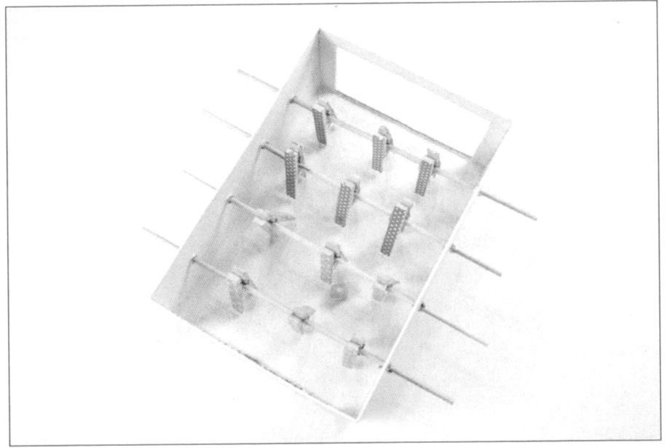

6 Tear off a long piece of washi tape. Roll it into a ball.

7 Use the washi tape ball to play a round of foosball.

8 Let the tournament begin!

SHOEBOX OVEN

The shoebox oven is the perfect craft to learn about science and the power of the sun. This project will also let you experiment with cooking yummy foods like s'mores, pizza, hot dogs and more! Just remember to always use precooked food. Your oven is used to just to heat and melt foods.

Age: 8+ with adult supervision

MATERIALS

- Shoebox with lid (make sure it's big enough to fit a small, disposable plate)
- Double-sided tape
- Scissors
- Aluminum foil
- Black paper
- Decorative paper or wrapping paper
- Clear plastic wrap
- Wooden skewer
- Tape

DIRECTIONS

1 Place double-sided tape all over the interior walls of the shoebox. Remove the backing from the tape so the sticky side is exposed.

2 Line the interior walls of the shoebox with aluminum foil, pressing down so it sticks to the tape. Do not cover the bottom of the box.

3 Add double-sided tape to the bottom of the box. Remove the backing from the tape so the sticky side is exposed.

4 Cover the bottom of the oven with black paper, pressing down so it sticks to the tape.

5 With the help of an adult, cut a three-sided flap from the lid of the shoebox, leaving at least a 1-inch border around the three sides.

6 Turn the lid over to see the inside. Use double-sided tape and place it next to the opening you just cut. Place the clear plastic on the tape to make a window.

7 Cover the flap with aluminum foil on the inside of the box. Use decorative paper to cover the top of the flap as well as the outside of the shoebox, if desired.

8 Pierce a hole on the flap with the skewer so it can prop open the flap, allowing the sun to shine through the box. Secure it with tape at the bottom.

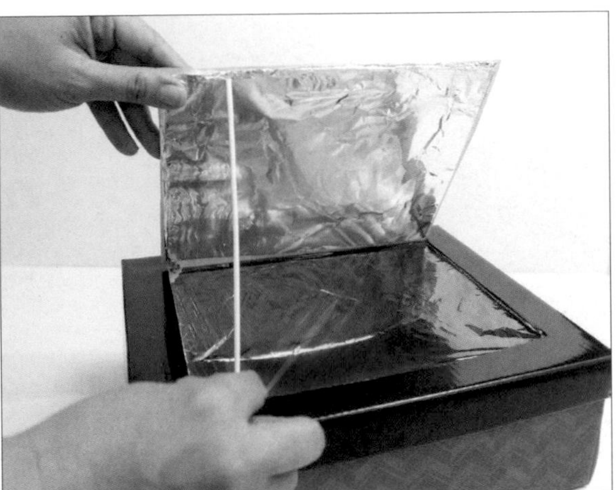

DUCT TAPE SHIELD & SWORD

Who knew tape could be so fun! Combine colorful tape with cardboard boxes for endless creative possibilities. This project will make you want to turn the television off and play outside for hours!

Age: 6+

MATERIALS

- Large cardboard box
- Scissors or box cutter
- Marker
- 2–3 rolls of colored duct tape

DIRECTIONS

1 Break down the large box and place it on a flat surface. Using scissors or a box cutter, cut off the two largest sides of the box.

2 With the marker, draw the shape of a shield on one piece of cardboard and a sword on the other piece.

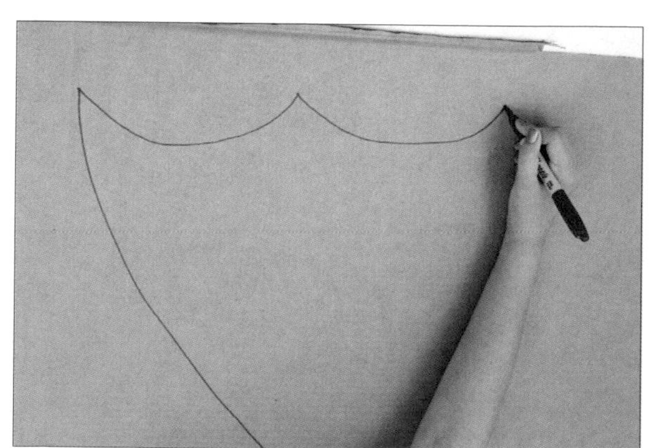

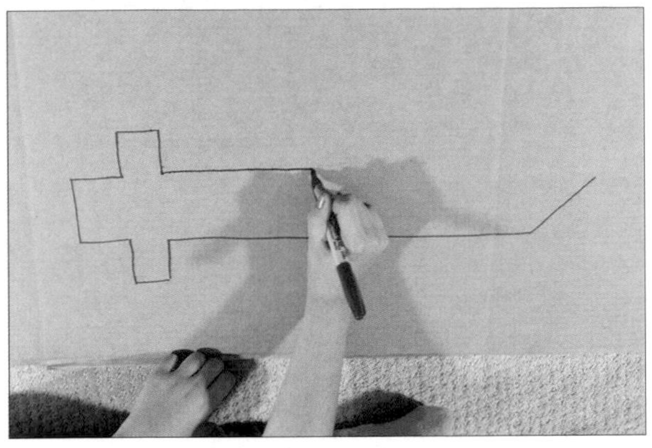

3 Cut out the shield and sword shapes with scissors or a box cutter. An adult may need to do this step for younger children.

4 Decorate one side of the cardboard shield with your duct tape. You can make a pattern with different colors of duct tape or markers. We like to decorate the entire surface of the shield with duct tape to make it sturdier.

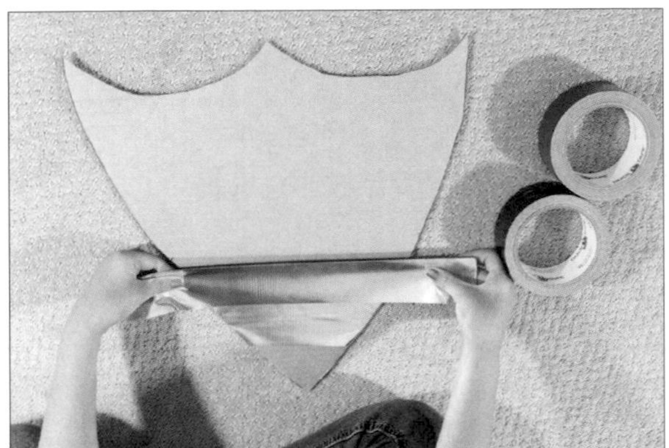

5 To make the shield's handle, cut two 6-inch pieces of duct tape and place the sticky sides together to form a double-ply handle. Horizontally secure the handle about a third of the way from the bottom using duct tape, making sure to leave a loop to hold the shield.

6 Grab a friend and let the duel begin!

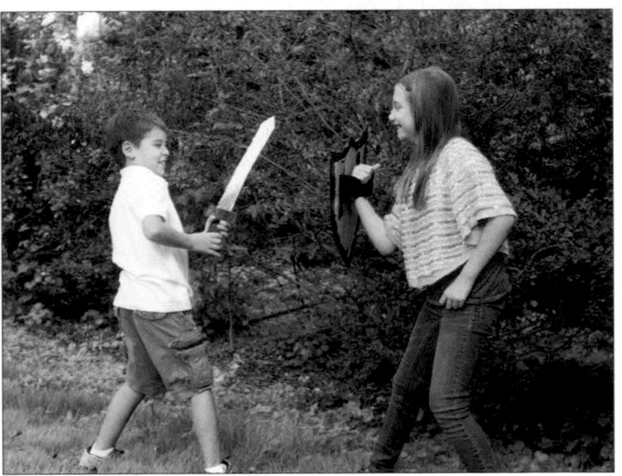

SUPERHERO CAPE & CUFFS

You can be a superhero with this supertastically easy no-sew cape and cuffs. Whether you are a superhero for Halloween or just want to save the world on Wednesday, you'll love it so much, you'll zoom away as soon as it's done!

Age: 8+

MATERIALS

- 28 x 18-inch piece of red fabric
- Fabric glue
- 30 inches of blue ribbon
- Stencils
- Marker
- Felt fabric in various colors
- Scissors
- Ruler
- 12 x 3 inches of red fabric
- Empty Toilet Paper Roll
- Hole Punch
- Excess Blue Felt
- (2) 6-inch pieces of thin ribbon

DIRECTIONS

For Cape:

1 Lay out the large piece of 28 x 18-inch red fabric on a flat surface.

2 Fold the 18-inch side of the red fabric over 2 inches and glue the open edge to the fabric to create a loop. You will be fishing your blue ribbon through there.

3 Once the fabric glue is dry, fish the blue ribbon through the loop you just created.

4 Using your stencils and marker, trace the designs and letters on the various pieces of felt fabric. Use the scissors to cut them out. We suggest writing your name and drawing a big lightening bolt.

5 Using the fabric glue, attach the shapes and letters to your cape. Be sure to only dab the glue to the center of your letters and shapes. Press it lightly in place to secure the felt. Add glue to the edges of the felt pieces to fully secure them.

For Cuffs:

1 Cut the toilet paper roll in half.

2 Cut the roll open.

3 Cut the red fabric in half so it measures 6 x 3 inches.

4 Cut the corners off each corner of the fabric.

5 Place the half of the toilet paper roll on the piece of fabric

6 Place glue around the edges of the fabric and fold over on to the toilet paper roll and hold each edge down to dry for at least 5 minutes.

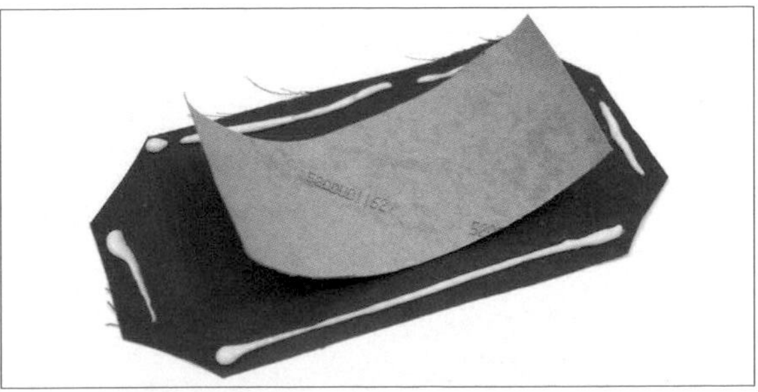

7 Once all the sides are dry punch a hole using the hole punch at each end of the cuff.

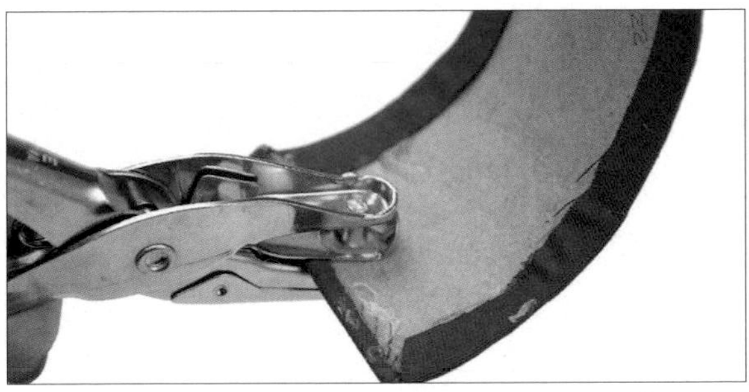

8 Flip cuff over and use fabric glue to attach the blue felt shapes.

9 String the ribbon through holes to use to secure the cuff to your wrist.

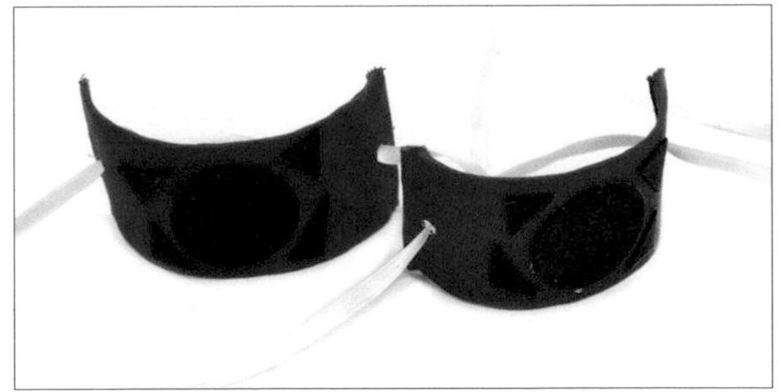

10 Repeat steps 4–9 for the second cuff.

ROBOT BOX HEAD

Boxes were one of our favorite things to play with when we were little. There are so many possibilities that can come from one brown, boring cardboard box. All you need is a little imagination. One of our favorite projects is a robot box head made with a few simple craft supplies. Feel free to add your own twist to this robot!

Age: 6+ with adult supervision

MATERIALS

- Marker
- Cardboard box
- Scissors
- Washi tape
- Pipe cleaners in different colors

DIRECTIONS

1 Using the marker, draw a mouth and eyes on the front of the box.

2 With help from an adult, use the scissors to cut the openings out for the mouth and the eyes.

3 Poke two holes on each side of the box so that they line up.

4 Insert one end of a pipe cleaner in one hole and the other end in the other hole to make the ear. Do the same on the other side of the box.

5 Poke a bunch of holes on the top of the box.

6 Insert a variety of colorful pipe cleaners through the holes on the top of the box, twisting and turning them to give your robot funky hair.

7 Outline the mouth and the eyes with the washi tape.

8 Slip on your box head and you are ready to start the robot party!

PILLOWCASE DECORATION

Bedtime will be anything but boring with this pillowcase craft. Use your creative juices to design your own pillowcase with ribbons. Make it match your sheets and display it on your bed for everyone to see. It might also bring you sweet dreams if you go to bed on time for mom and dad!

Age: 7+

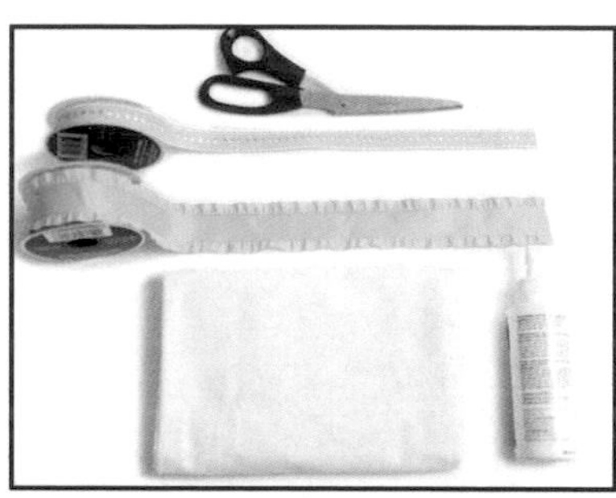

MATERIALS

- 1 pillow
- 1 white pillowcase
- 1 spool thick ribbon
- Scissors
- 1 spool thin ribbon
- Fabric glue

DIRECTIONS

1 Slip your pillow into the white pillowcase. Lay the pillow flat on a table.

2 Take your thick ribbon and use it to measure across the short side of the pillow.

3 Cut it to stretch the length.

4 Use the thick ribbon to measure and cut the length of the thin ribbon.

5 Using the fabric glue, attach the thin piece of ribbon to run across the center of the thick ribbon.

6 Flip the thick ribbon over.

7 Add a few drops of glue across the back of the thick ribbon.

8 With the glue side down, gently place the ribbon across the width of the pillowcase, about 2 inches from the opening edge.

9 Allow it to dry for five minutes.

10 Cut a 10-inch piece of thick ribbon, a 10-inch piece of thin ribbon and a 3-inch piece of thin ribbon.

11 Using the fabric glue, attach the 10-inch piece of ribbon to run across the center of the thick ribbon.

12 Dab both ends of the longer, double-ribbon piece with fabric glue and glue the ends together so that the ribbon makes a circle. Allow it to dry for five minutes.

13 With the glued pieces in the center of your ribbon circle, press it together with your fingers to form a bow.

14 Take the smaller piece of ribbon, add some glue and wrap it around to secure the center of the bow.

15 Let the bow dry for 15–20 minutes.

16 Once the bow is dry, add a generous glob of glue to the center back of the bow and glue it to the corner of the pillow.

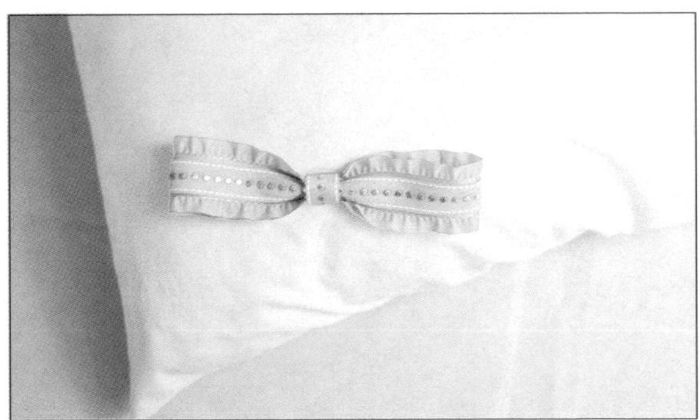

FLEECE BLANKET

There's no better way to stay warm on a chilly night than with a soft fleece blanket with fun fringe edges. This easy no-sew blanket can be whipped up in under 30 minutes and is a great project to practice coordination and creative design. Pick a fun fleece that matches your bedroom. Cozy up and snuggle under a blanket made with love!

Age: 8+

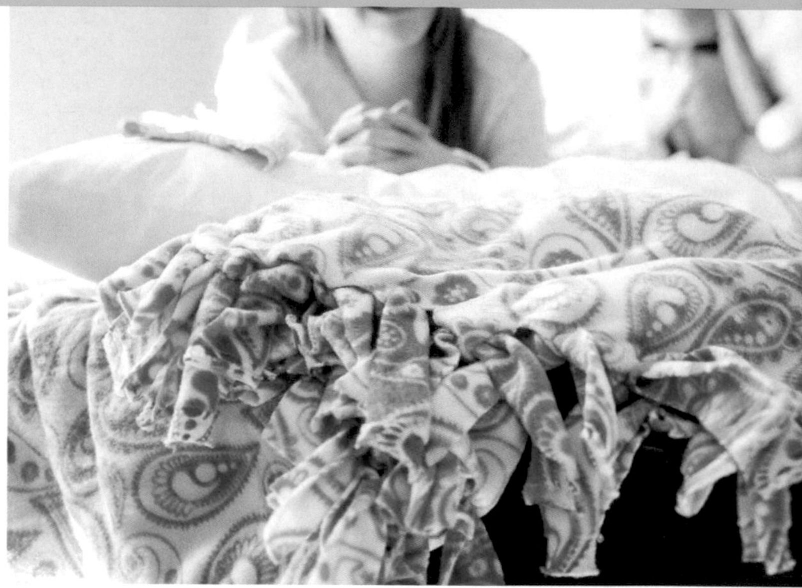

MATERIALS

- 2 yards of fleece—color one
- 2 yards of fleece—color two
- Scissors
- Ruler

DIRECTIONS

1 Lay fleece color one flat facedown and lay fleece color 2 face up on top of it.

2 Cut two 5-inch squares out of each corner of the fleece fabrics.

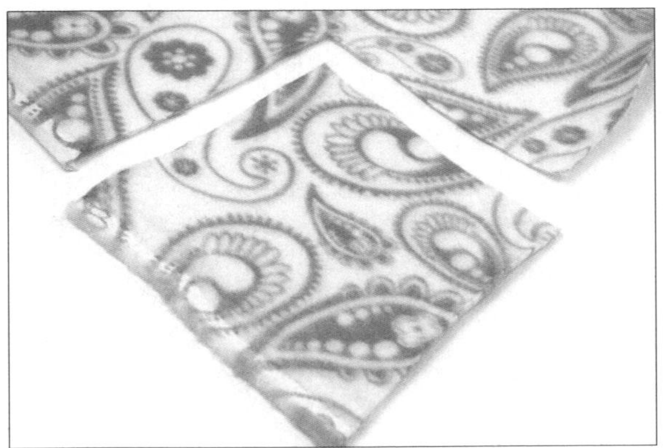

3 Next, cut 5-inch-deep strips into the edges of the fleece, spacing them about an inch apart. Do this all the way around all four sides. It will look like fringe.

4 Take the top and bottom of each strip and tie them together using a double knot. Do this on all four sides until all the strips are tied into knots.

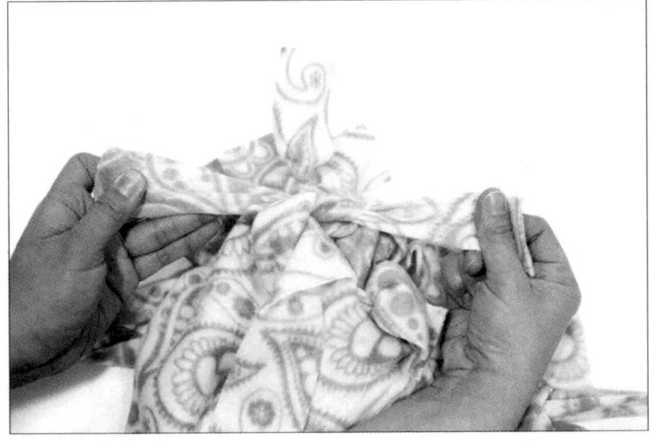

5 Ta-da—you now have your own custom blanket. Time to snuggle by the fire!

NO-SEW PLAYTIME PILLOW

Whether you are fighting with them or relaxing on one while reading a book, pillows are so much fun! I bet you never thought you could easily make one. This simple no-sew pillow can be made pretty quickly and used for relaxing in the playroom or decorating your bedroom.

Age: 6+

MATERIALS

- 1 piece of 24 x 24-inch fabric
- Fabric glue
- Pillow stuffing

DIRECTIONS

1 Lay fabric out on a flat surface with the pattern facing up.

2 Fold the fabric in half so the back side is facing up.

3 Open the edges and place a small amount of glue along the front side edges, leaving 4 inches at the end unglued.

4 Let the glue dry for at least one hour.

5 Once the glue is dry, flip the fabric through the unglued opening.

6 Place the pillow stuffing into the opening of the pillow. Stuff as little or as much as you want based on how fluffy you want the pillow.

7 Fold the top and bottom of the edges inward and use fabric glue to glue it shut. Hold the seam for a few minutes or use clothespins to keep it shut.

8 Let the seam dry for at least one hour.

9 Wait at least seven days before washing.

HOMEMADE SLEEPOVER TENT

Camp out in your room and hide away in your own A-Tent. Or, round out the perfect slumber party with custom tents. Adults will need to lead this project, but you can help pick out the fabric and the decorations for the tent.

Age: Adult with a special helper

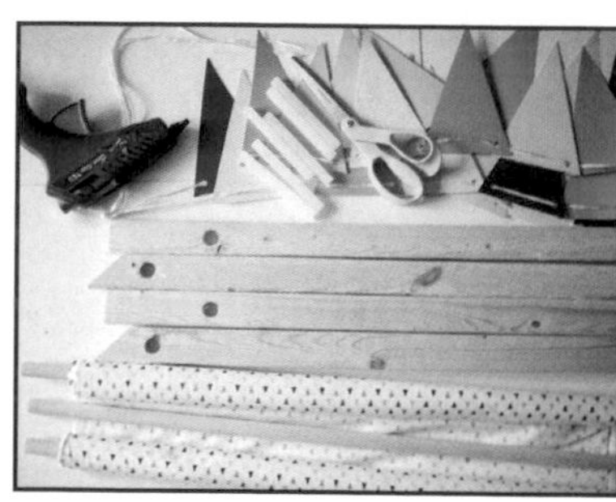

MATERIALS

- (2) 1 x 2 x 8-inch wood boards
- 120-grit sandpaper
- Power drill with ⅝-inch spade drill bit
- Ruler or measuring tape
- Scissors
- 2½ yards of fabric
- Hot glue gun
- (3) ⅝ x 36-inch wooden dowels
- Paper pennant garland

DIRECTIONS

1 When purchasing the 1 x 2 x 8-inch boards, have the hardware store cut each board in half into 4-foot boards. Have them cut one end of each board at a 45-degree angle. These ends will be at the foot of the tent.

2 Use the sandpaper to smooth the rough edges of the boards to prevent splinters.

3 Drill a ⅝-inch hole 4 inches from the flat end of each board using the spade drill bit.

4 Drill a ⅝-inch hole 2 inches from the angled end of each board using the spade bit.

5 Measure and cut the fabric 30 inches wide and leave the length at 2½ yards.

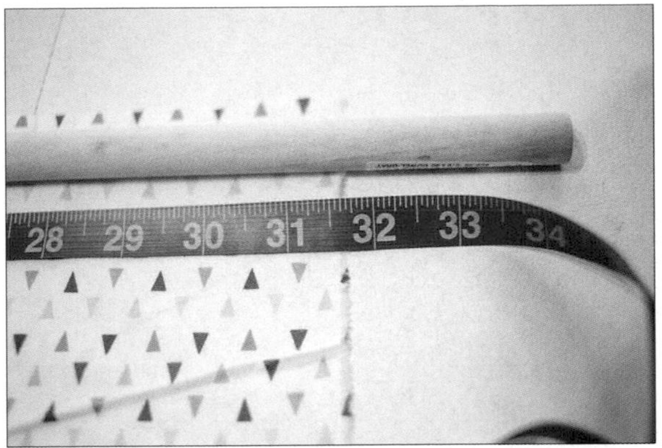

6 Using the hot glue gun, attach the first dowel to the end of the fabric, leaving 1½ inches on each end.

7 Roll the fabric along the dowel, and continue to hot glue the fabric to the dowel. Stop after three rotations.

8 Repeat at the other end of the fabric with the second dowel.

9 Set up the front of the A-tent by crossing two boards at the top. The angled foot should be at the bottom facing outward.

10 Insert one end of the third dowel at the top intersection where the ⅝-inch hole was made.

11 Set up the back of the A-tent the same way as the front. Insert the other end of the third dowel where the boards intersect.

12 Drape fabric with the dowel attached over the third dowel.

13 Insert the first and second dowel along the angled bottom hole on each end.

14 Roll the first or second dowel to tighten the fabric over the tent.

15 Decorate the tent with the paper pennant garland.

RIBBON DANCER WAND

Dance the day away with a magical ribbon dancer wand or pretend to be a fairy princess saving the enchanted land. A ribbon dancer wand and your imagination can take you anywhere your heart desires.

Age: 5+ with adult supervision

MATERIALS

- Scissors
- 3 colors of ¼-inch-wide ribbon
- 1 wooden dowel
- Hot glue gun
- Roll of washi tape

DIRECTIONS

1 Using the scissors, cut five pieces of each color ribbon to the length of the wooden stick.

2 With the help of an adult, carefully attach each piece of ribbon to one end of the stick using the hot glue gun.

3 Once the glue is dry, wrap the stick in washi tape, starting from the bottom and working your way to the top.

4 At the top, wrap the washi tape several times around the glued ends of the ribbon. Now dance away!

FLOWER PEN

Flower pens make writing more fun and stylish. When you are not writing, these flower pens can stay in a small vase to make the perfect flower arrangement for your desk, room or next tea party.

Age: 8+

MATERIALS

- Pen
- Silk flower with stem
- Wire cutter
- Green floral tape
- Body spray or perfume

DIRECTIONS

1 Line up the pen and stem of the flower. If the flower stem is longer than the pen, cut the stem with the wire cutter so it is a little shorter.

2 Hold the pen and stem together.

3 Starting at right about the tip of the pen, wrap the green floral tape around the pen and the floral stem as tight as possible.

4 Once you get to the top of the pen and the base of the flower, tear off the excess green floral tape.

5 Spritz your flower pen with body spray or perfume to give it a fun scent like a real flower!

PARTY TIME

ACCORDION NOTEBOOK

For trading notes, writing stories and drawing pictures, a notebook can bring so much joy! Making a notebook from scratch is 10 times better and provides a great blank canvas to create and save memories. Encourage all the party guests to write or draw a story in their newly created notebook and share it with everyone before hitting the hay!

Age: 7+

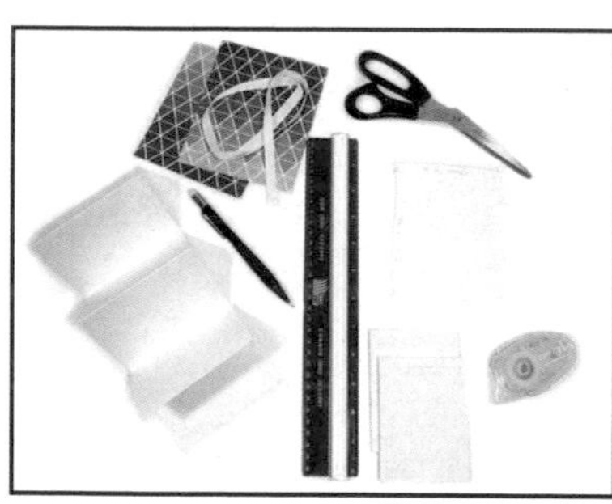

MATERIALS

- (2) 4½ x 5½-inch pieces of scrapbook paper
- (2) 3 x 4-inch foam board pieces
- Pencils
- Ruler
- Scissors
- 1 glue roller
- (1) 4 x 21-inch white poster board
- 2 feet of white ribbon
- Stamps, scrapbook stickers, or washi tape if you want to embellish

DIRECTIONS

1 Lay the first piece of scrapbook paper flat with the front facing down, and place the first foam board in the center. Use the pencil and the ruler to draw lines, and cut the corners off of each corner with scissors.

2 Roll the glue along the border of the foam board.

3 Fold the edges of the scrapbook paper over the foam board and press firmly.

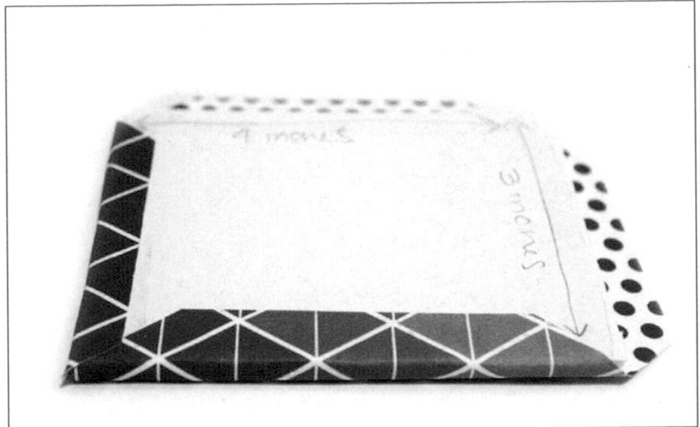

4 Repeat steps 1–3 for the other piece of scrapbook paper and foam board.

5 Fold the poster board every 3 inches, like an accordion, and set aside.

6 Roll a line of glue on the center of the back side of the foam board (exposed foam board facing up).

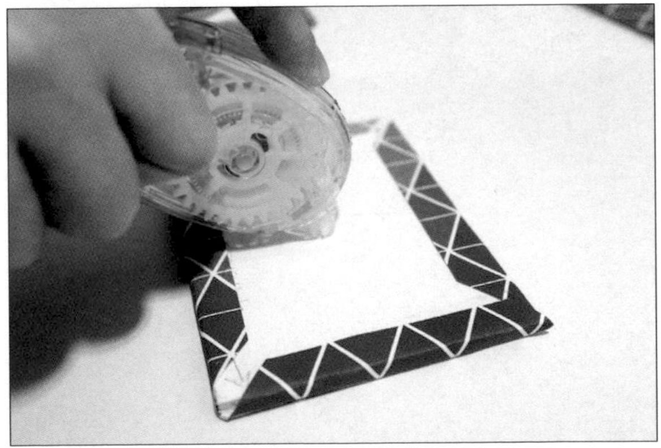

7 Fold ribbon in half, lay the center of the ribbon on the glue line and press firmly.

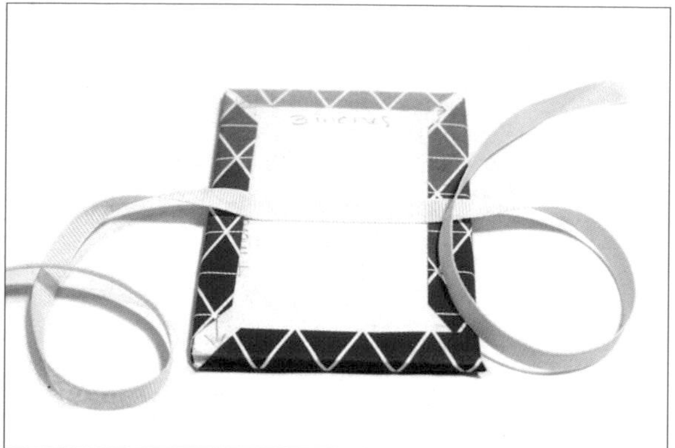

8 Cover the exposed foam board with glue.

9 Press the poster board accordion firmly on the foam board and hold for 10–15 seconds.

10 Repeat step 8 with the other foam piece and connect to the other end of the accordion.

11 If you want to embellish, use stamps, scrapbook stickers or washi tape.

12 Tie ribbon around the book in a bow.

HOMEMADE HEADBAND

At ballerina recitals and at home playing dress up, a fancy headband will complete your perfect outfit. This easy craft will help you feel as special as a princess. You might need a little help from mom with the hot glue gun.

Age: 6+ with adult supervision

MATERIALS

- Hot glue gun
- Rhinestones
- Plain plastic or fabric headband
- Feathers or flowers

DIRECTIONS

1 Using the hot glue gun, affix rhinestones one by one across the first two-thirds of the headband.

2 Leave a 2-inch space with no rhinestones and continue to glue the rhinestones until you get to the end of the headband.

3 Allow glue to dry for five minutes.

4 Once the glue has dried, glue your feathers or flowers to the designated empty spot. Use a generous amount of glue.

5 Allow it to dry completely before playing dress up.

FISHING GAME

Let's go fishing! Have endless fun catching colorful fish with your very own fishing rod. No water needed, only imagination, a few supplies and friends to fish with! This great craft will teach you hand-eye coordination and counting. It is a great project that will keep on giving and teaching valuable skills.

Age: 4+ with adult supervision

MATERIALS

- 2 screw eyes
- 1⅝ x 36-inch dowel
- Hot glue gun
- Thread spool
- 1 acorn dowel cap
- (5) 9 x 12-inch felt fabric sheets in a variety of colors
- Black permanent marker
- Scissors
- Heavy-duty adhesive back magnetic tape
- (1) 9 x 12-inch white felt fabric sheet
- 2 yards of thin cotton cord
- 1 nickel
- Mini thread spool
- Medium bucket

DIRECTIONS

1 Have your an adult help you insert the first screw eye into the top of the dowel. Turn the screw eye to tighten the hold. Repeat with the second screw eye in the middle of the dowel.

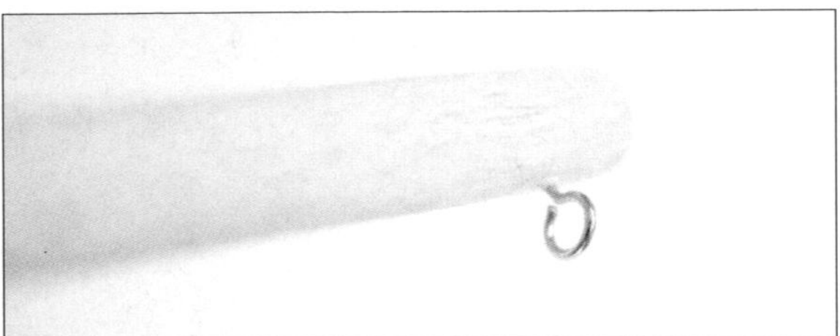

2 Hot glue the thread spool 8 inches from the end of the dowel. Let glue cool for five minutes.

3 Hot glue the acorn dowel cap to the end of the thread spool. Let glue cool for five minutes.

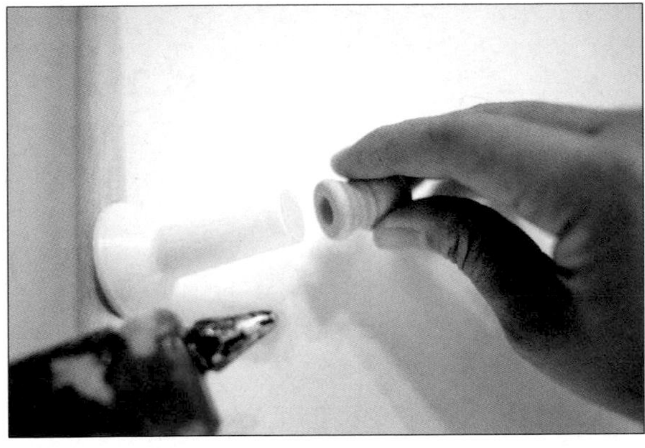

4 Fold a felt fabric sheet in half. Draw two fish using the black permanent marker. Use the scissors to cut it out. Repeat this for all five felt fabrics.

5 Cut a strip of heavy-duty magnetic tape and stick it to the inside lining of the felt fish. Do this for all of the fish.

6 Hot glue the top layer of the fish to hide the magnetic strip inside each fish. Let the glue cool for five minutes.

7 Cut a strip of white felt long enough to cover the bottom of the dowel.

8 Hot glue the white felt by rolling it along the dowel.

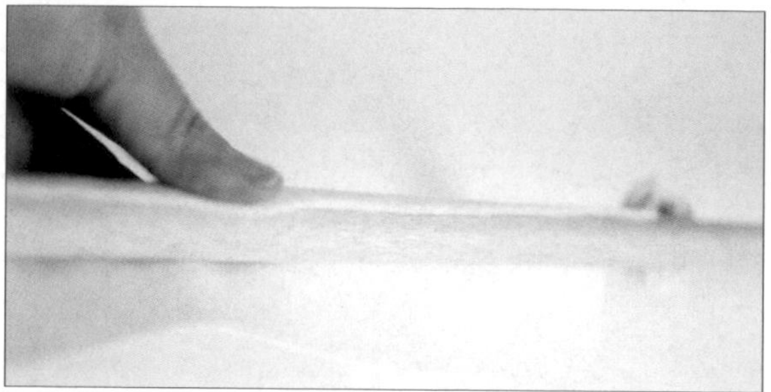

9 Loop the cotton cord through the screw eye and twist the remaining cord along the thread spool.

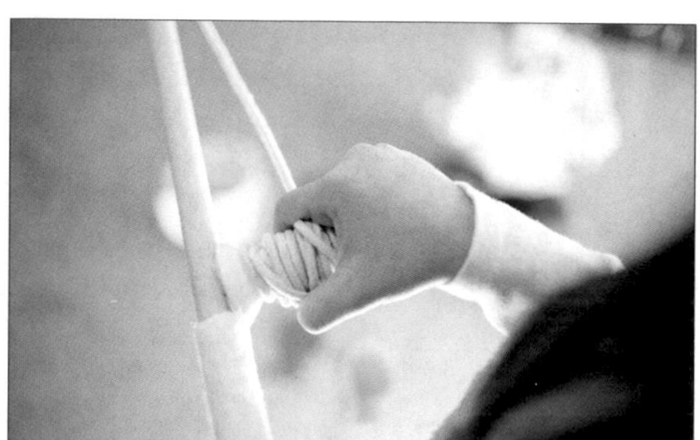

10 Hot glue the nickel to the flat surface of the mini thread spool.

11 Fill the inner tube of the mini spool with hot glue. Tuck the end of the cord into the inner tube. Let the glue cool and dry completely (5 minutes).

12 Grab a bucket, lay your fish on the floor and start fishing. Catch the fish by touching them to the end of your fishing pole string.

RAIN STICK

The rain forest is music to our ears. You can create the rain forest sounds and make your very own rain stick at home with a few simple supplies and a little creative imagination.

Age: 10+

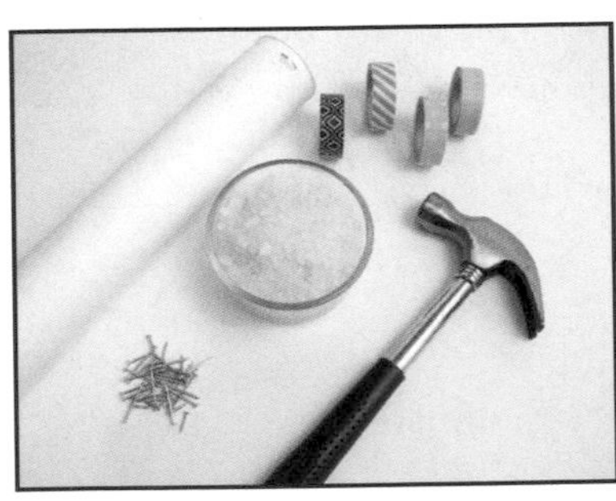

MATERIALS

- (1) 2 x 18-inch packing tube
- Hammer
- (18) 1-inch nails
- Decorative tape
- 2 cups of ice cream salt

DIRECTIONS

1 Use the hammer to slowly tap the nails into the packing tube sporadically around, up and down the tube. Place nails at least 3 inches apart.

2 Decorate the outside of the tube with decorative tape to add your own creative touch. Stripes are our favorite.

3 Open one end of the tube by twisting off the top.

4 Fill the tube with the ice cream salt.

5 Secure the top and turn your rain stick upside down to hear the tropical magic!

GUITAR

Turn a simple tissue box into your very own music machine. This simple guitar craft will let you pretend to be a rockstar or country star. All you need is a little imagination!

Age: 7+ with adult supervision

MATERIALS

- 1 rectangular tissue box
- Elmer's glue or hot glue gun
- 2 Popsicle sticks
- Pencil
- 1 paper towel or cardboard wrapping paper tube
- Box cutter
- 1 piece of scrapbook paper
- Tape (optional)
- 6 extra-large rubber bands
- Scissors
- 6 pushpins

DIRECTIONS

1 Remove the clear plastic around the opening in the tissue box.

2 Glue Popsicle sticks at the ends of each of the openings and let dry for 5–10 minutes. (If using a hot glue gun, have an adult supervise.)

3 With a pencil, trace the end of the tube on the side of the tissue box. Have an adult cut out the circle with a box cutter.

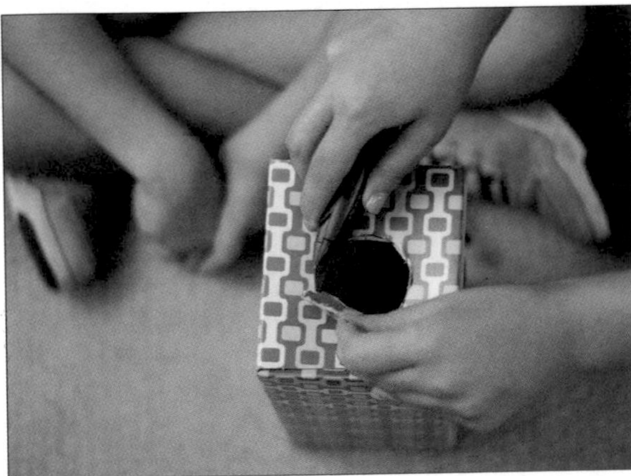

4 Wrap the tube with scrapbook paper and secure with glue or tape.

5 Stretch three extra-large rubber bands across the tube, resting the rubbers bands on the flat end of each tube. The rubber bands will be stretched tight so they will stay in place on their own.

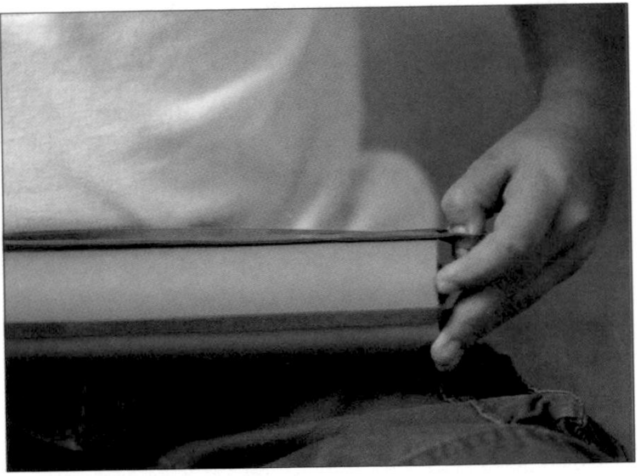

6 Using the scissors, cut the remaining rubber bands a little longer than the length of the opening in the tissue box.

7 Stretch the cut rubber bands from one Popsicle stick to the other, securing each end with a pushpin. Make sure the rubber bands are stretched tight.

8 Insert the tube in the circular hole cut on the side of the tissue box.

9 You now have a homemade guitar!

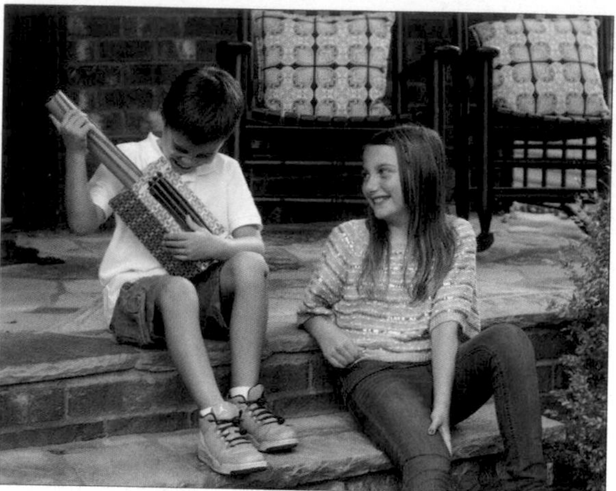

MARACAS

Now that you have your guitar and rain stick, add a little Spanish music to your band. Shake, shake, shake to create fun sounds and your own songs!

Age: 4+

MATERIALS

- Plastic Easter eggs
- 1 tablespoon of uncooked rice
- Even number of plastic spoons
- Clear tape

DIRECTIONS

1 Open the Easter egg and fill it with the 1 tablespoon of uncooked rice. Close the egg.

2 Set the egg in the mouth of one of the plastic spoons and place the other spoon on top of the egg.

3 Hold the spoons tight so the egg does not fall. Secure enough tape around the handles of the spoons so the egg does not fall out of the spoons.

4 You are ready to make music!

VALENTINE'S DAY LOVE ARROWS

Lovestruck is the name of the game with these cute arrows for Valentine's Day. Cupid would be proud of your creative arrows made from sticks in your backyard!

Age: 7+

MATERIALS

- Pencil
- Scissors
- Red and pink construction paper
- Hot glue gun
- Sticks from your backyard
- 3 feathers
- Yarn

DIRECTIONS

1 Using your pencil and scissors, draw and cut a heart out of the red construction paper.

2 Draw and cut out a smaller heart on the pink construction paper.

3 Glue the small heart to the big heart with the hot glue gun.

4 Using the hot glue gun, attach the heart to the end of the stick.

5 Take the three feathers and use the hot glue gun to attach them to the opposite end of the stick.

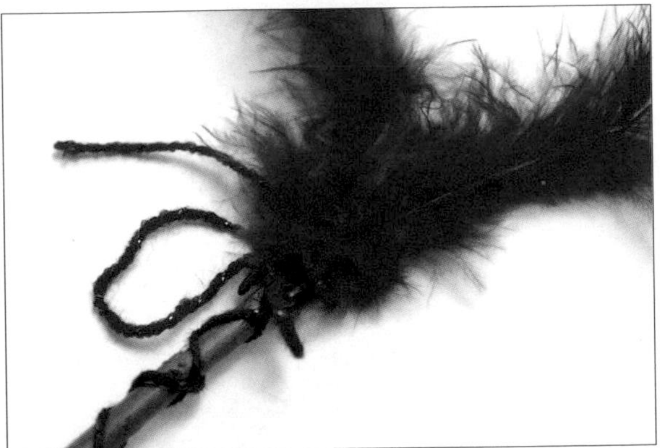

6 Turn the heart over so the back where it is glued to the stick is facing upward.

7 Cut two pieces of yarn one-and-a-half times the length of your stick.

8 Using the glue gun, attach each end of the yarn to the back of the heart, on either side of the stick.

9 Wrap both pieces around the stick in an alternating fashion to create a crisscross pattern.

10 Tie a knot and a bow really tight at the top of the stick.

11 Trim off the excess yarn.

12 Ta-da! You have an arrow cupid would be proud of.

VALENTINE'S DAY GARLAND

Valentine's Day is a day of love, friendship, lots of sweets and pretty decorations. Decorate your room or help your teacher decorate the classroom with this easy Valentine's Day playing card garland. This project is so festive you could keep it up all year long!

Age: 8+

MATERIALS

- Hole punch
- Deck of playing cards
- 5 feet of red ribbon
- Assorted 12-inch pieces of red, pink, and white ribbons

DIRECTIONS

1 Punch two holes at the top of every card in the deck. Make the holes about 1 inch apart.

2 String your cards on the 5-foot red ribbon by weaving the ribbon in and out of the holes.

3 Space the cards a few inches apart.

4 Lay your string of cards out on a table.

5 Tie your 12-inch pieces of ribbon to the garland in between the cards, varying the colors. You can do as few or as many ribbons as you see fit.

ST. PATRICK'S DAY PENCIL ART

Rainbows, leprechauns, shamrocks, and pots of gold are the mysteries that make St. Patrick's Day so fun. Make your own shamrock art on kitchen towels so your parents can display them in the kitchen for everyone to see. Who knows, maybe a leprechaun will stop by and hide a pot of gold in your kitchen!

Age: 7+ with adult supervision

MATERIALS

- Iron
- Cotton flour sack towels
- Parchment paper
- Card stock cut in the shape of a shamrock
- Double-sided tape
- 3 standard number 2 pencils, with erasers
- 3 shades of green fabric paint
- White sheet or towels

DIRECTIONS

1 Have an adult iron your towels on a flat, clean, and heat-safe surface.

2 Cover a flat surface with parchment paper so you don't spill paint.

3 Lay towel flat on the parchment paper.

4 Secure your shamrock stencil to the towel with double-sided tape.

5 Take turns dipping your pencil erasers in the different color paints and stamping dots around the stencil.

6 Once complete, let the towel dry for four to six hours.

7 To seal the paint, lay the towel on a heat-safe surface, cover with a white sheet or towels and have an adult run a hot iron over the sheet a few times.

8 Wash as you normally would wash other towels.

YARN EASTER EGGS

The Easter Bunny usually just leaves boring plastic eggs. Show the Easter Bunny your creative skills with these free-formed yarn Easter eggs. They are so fun to make and great for display. You can also add a string and tie them on a ribbon to make a garland.

Age: 5+

MATERIALS

- Parchment paper
- Balloons
- Foam brush
- Mod Podge
- Yarn
- Scissors
- Tweezers (optional)

DIRECTIONS

1 Cover a work surface with parchment paper.

2 Blow up the balloons about one-fourth the size they normally would be if they were fully blown up. They will have the shape of eggs.

3 Using the foam brush, cover the entire balloon with Mod Podge.

4 Take your yarn and wrap it around the balloon. Keep wrapping and going multiple ways until you have the egg about half covered with yarn.

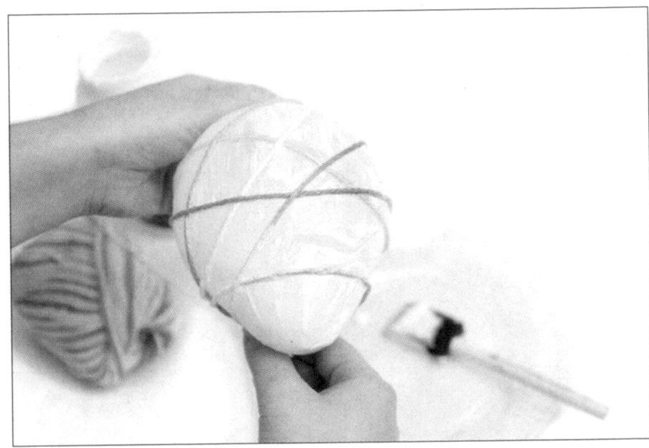

5 Using your brush, spread more Mod Podge over the yarn. Use your finger to add a big drop to stick the end and beginning of the yarn to the balloon.

6 Set the balloon on the parchment paper to dry for one to two hours.

7 Once the balloon is dry, pop it with scissors and use your fingers or tweezers to pull the deflated balloon out of the egg.

8 Repeat steps 3–7 on all of the balloons.

{ HOLIDAYS }

CHOCOLATE BUNNY POPS

Marshmallow Peeps have been a long-time favorite and tradition for Easter celebrations. The only thing that will make the sugary Peeps tastier is dipping them in chocolate. These are fun treats to set out for the Easter Bunny. Celebrate Easter this year with a fun, festive and chocolatey twist!

Age: 10+

MATERIALS

- Parchment paper
- 10-ounce package of milk chocolate chips
- Large microwave-safe bowl
- Pot holder
- Spoon
- 6 marshmallow bunny Peeps
- 6 decorative paper straws
- 6 small marshmallows
- Sprinkles
- ½ dozen cardboard egg carton
- Scissors
- Clear plastic wrap (optional)
- Ribbon (optional)

DIRECTIONS

1 Line the countertop or a table with parchment paper.

2 Pour chocolate chips into the microwave-safe bowl.

3 Microwave the chocolate for 30 seconds at a time. After each 30 seconds, remove the bowl using a pot holder and stir the chocolate with a spoon.

4 Continue to microwave in 30-second increments until the chocolate is completely melted and smooth.

5 While you are microwaving the chocolate, push the straws into the bunny Peeps to create bunny pops.

6 Once the chocolate is melted, hold your bunny pops and dip them far enough into the melted chocolate to cover most of the bunny.

7 Lay the chocolate-dipped bunny pops flat on the parchment paper.

8 Repeat steps 5 and 6 for the remaining bunnies.

9 Add a marshmallow to each bunny to form the tail.

10 Lightly shake sprinkles over the chocolate bunnies.

11 Let the chocolate bunnies dry for one hour.

12 While the bunnies are drying, take the cardboard egg carton, turn it upside down and use the scissors to punch small holes in each egg section.

13 When the bunny pops are dry, push the straws into each section of the egg carton to create a fun display.

14 If you want to give the bunny pops to your friends, you can wrap the top of each bunny pop with clear plastic wrap and tie shut with a ribbon.

JULY 4TH LANTERNS

Fireworks and barbecues are some of our favorite things about summer. Celebrate the USA by helping your parents make the house festive. These paper lanterns are so easy and will add the perfect touch to any celebration or just to decorate your room.

Age: 7+

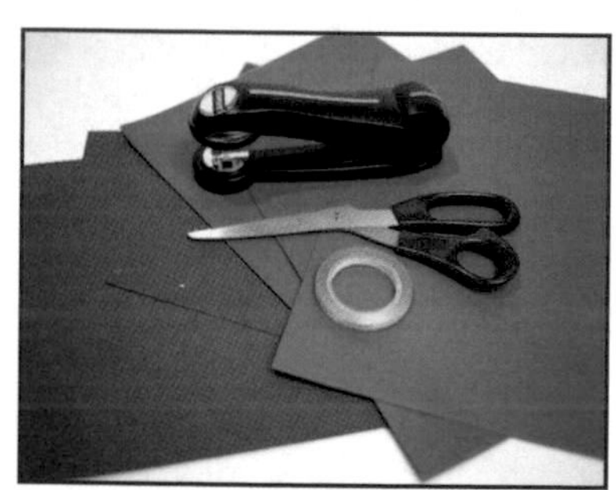

MATERIALS

- (4) 8½ x 11-inch sheet of red construction paper
- Scissors
- (4) 8½ x 11-inch sheet of blue construction paper
- Stapler
- Silver glitter tape
- String

DIRECTIONS

1 Fold one red piece of construction paper in half hamburger style.

2 Using the scissors, make a 4-inch cut 1 inch from the end. Make the cut from the folded side toward the open end.

3 Repeat step 2, making cuts 1 inch part.

4 Repeat steps 1–3 on the remaining pieces of construction paper.

5 Open up the hamburger fold and roll it like a hot dog, securing the top and bottom of the lantern with a stapler.

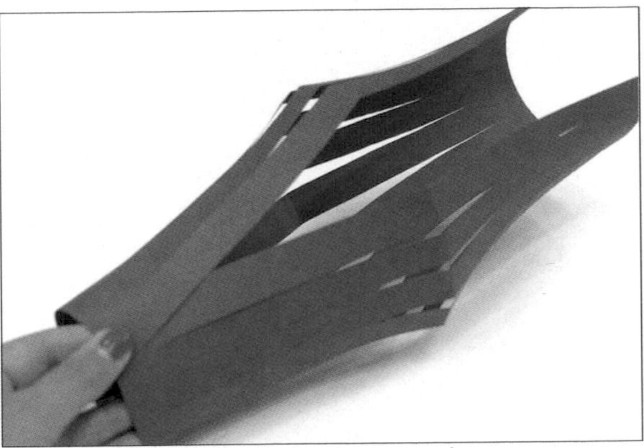

6 Decorate the top and bottom edges of the lantern with the silver glitter tape.

7 Cut two 3-inch strips of tape and stick them together to create a hook for the top of the lantern.

8 Using the hook you created in step 7, secure each end inside the top of the lantern with small pieces of tape. You are finishing the hook to hang the lantern.

9 Repeat steps 5–8 for the remaining sheets of construction paper.

10 Once all the lanterns are complete, string and hang indoors or outdoors to get ready for July 4th festivities.

GLOW-IN-THE-DARK SPIDER WEB

Be the coolest house in the neighborhood on Halloween with the biggest and scariest glow-in-the-dark spider web. This is a fun activity to get your whole family crafting.

Age: Easy for any age with help from the whole family

MATERIALS

- 100 feet of twine
- Scissors
- Mini hooks with adhesive tabs
- Glow-in-the-dark paint
- Paintbrush
- 2 glow-in-the-dark spiders

DIRECTIONS

1 Cut nine pieces of twine 4 feet long. This will be used for the base of the web.

2 Line up the nine pieces of twine and tie a knot at the very end. Trim off the excess twine.

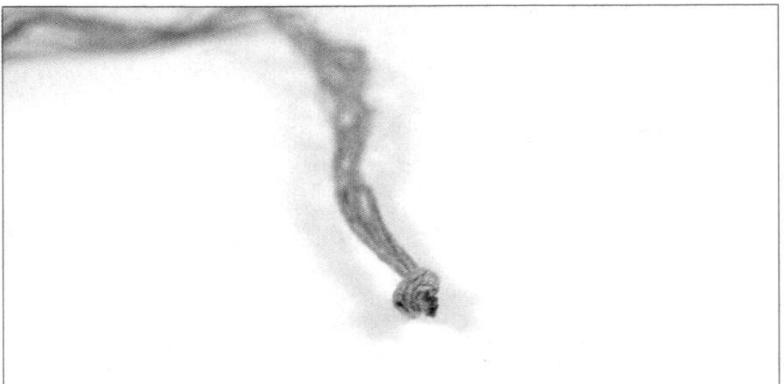

3 Spread the twine and tie a knot every 1 inch of each piece, starting from the big knot outward. These knots will hold the web connections in place.

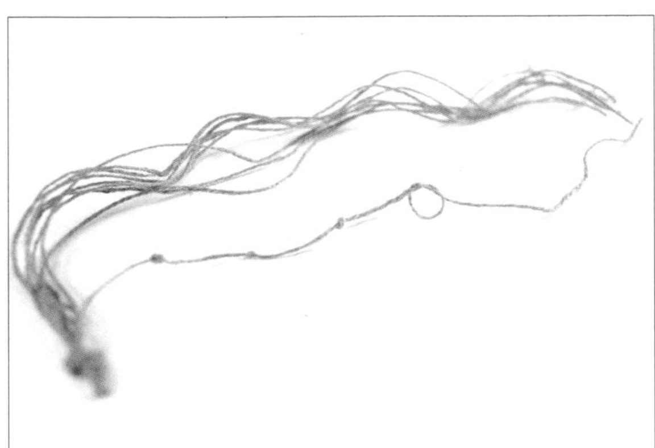

4 Stick a mini hook to a wall or a tree where you want to hang the web.

5 Place the eight other hooks in the area in a circular (asterisk) format.

6 After all nine strings are knotted, spread the strings out and tie each to a mini hook. It should look like a giant asterisk.

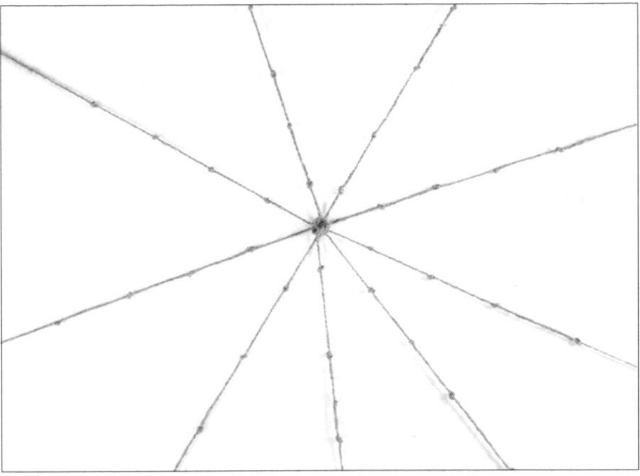

7 Starting from the center, loop the twine around each of the knots going in a spiral pattern around the web. Stop when half of the web is finished.

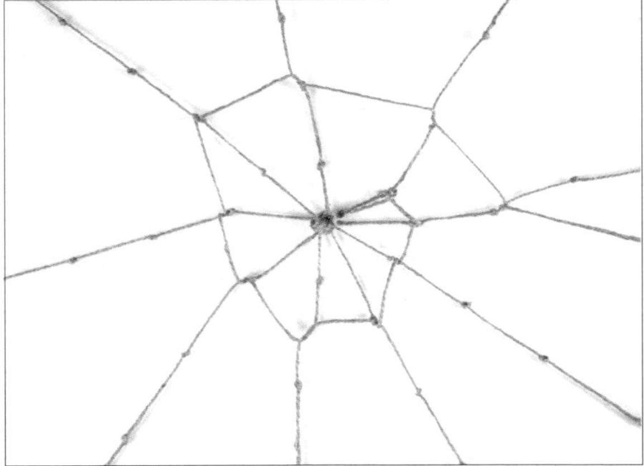

8 Paint the twine with glow-in-the dark paint using the paintbrush.

9 Add the glow-in-the-dark spiders by tucking each one into the web.

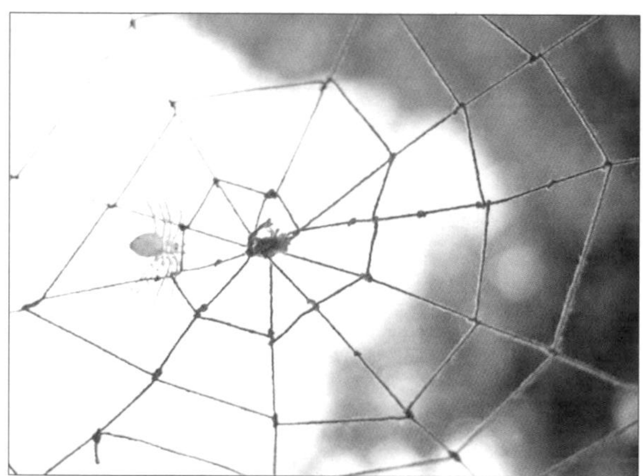

10 Activate the glow-in-the-dark paint by shinning a light onto the web for five minutes.

11 Turn off the light or wait for it to get dark and watch the web glow!

THANKFUL TREE

Giving thanks is a big part of the holiday season. It's also important to be thankful year round. This fun and easy Thankful Tree will allow you and your family to display and talk about all the wonderful things you are thankful for.

Age: 7+ with adult supervision

MATERIALS

- Branches from your yard (about 1½–2 feet long)
- Hot glue gun
- Tin bucket
- Permanent marker
- Fall-colored paper
- Scissors
- Hole punch
- String
- Tissue or shredded paper

DIRECTIONS

1 Using the hot glue gun, glue the bottom of the branches to the bottom of the tin bucket. Hold the branches in place so they are standing up until the glue dries (5 minutes). You may need to add lots of glue for them to stand up. Add shredded paper or tissue in the bucket to cover the base of the branches.

2 Draw leaf shapes with the permanent marker on the paper, and cut them out with the scissors.

3 Punch a hole at the end of each leaf.

4 Cut 5 inches of string for each leaf.

5 Write what you are thankful for on each leaf. Share leaves with your family and ask them to write what they are thankful for.

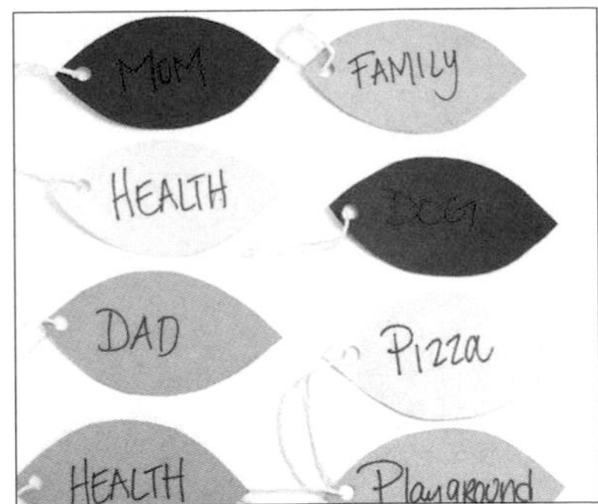

6 Tie each leaf to a branch on the tree and display it so the whole family can be reminded of everything they are thankful for!

SALT DOUGH ORNAMENT

Let the holiday celebrations begin! Make your own Christmas tree ornaments from simple kitchen ingredients. You will be able to proudly display these on the tree (or give them away as gifts) and tell all your friends exactly how you created them.

Age: 5+ with adult supervision

MATERIALS

- 2 cups flour
- ¾ cup salt
- ½ cup of water
- Large mixing bowl
- Cookie cutters
- Baking pan
- Parchment paper
- Plastic straw
- Acrylic paint
- Paintbrush
- Ribbon

DIRECTIONS

1 Preheat the oven to 275°F.

2 Mix the flour, salt and water in a large mixing bowl to make the dough.

3 After everything is mixed, flour a clean, dry surface and roll the dough out flat to a ½-inch thickness.

4 Stamp out the desired ornament shape using a cookie cutter.

5 Cover a baking pan with parchment paper.

6 Place the ornament onto the parchment-lined tray.

7 Using the straw, make a hole at the top of the ornament for the ribbon later.

8 Place tray in the oven and bake for two to three hours until completely dry. Remove and let cool.

9 Decorate the ornament with acrylic paint and a paintbrush.

10 Let the paint dry for 30 minutes.

11 Once the paint is dry, tie a piece of 5-inch ribbon to the ornament and let the holiday decorating begin!

Note: Keep the ornament away from any four-legged animals. The amount of salt in these ornaments can be toxic if digested.

BUTTON CANVAS ART

Button up a great work of art with a little painter's tape, festive buttons and paint. Create your own shapes or write a message. The more creative the design, the more special the work of art will be to hang on your wall.

Age: 10+

MATERIALS

- Scrap newspaper
- Painter's tape
- 11 x 14-inch canvas
- Blue paint
- Foam brush
- Pencil
- Variety of 50–60 buttons (you can use a mix of colors and sizes)
- School glue

DIRECTIONS

1 Cover a flat surface with newspaper so you don't make the dinner table a work of art!

2 Stretch the painter's tape across the canvas horizontally, and use your hand to press down firmly.

3 Add more strips of tape, leaving 1½ inches of canvas space between each tape strip. Make sure to press firmly so they stick to the canvas.

4 Paint the blank canvas between the strips of tape using the foam brush.

5 Go outside and play for 30 minutes while the paint dries.

6 Peel away the tape. You will be amazed by the straight lines!

7 Use your pencil to lightly draw a heart in the center of the canvas.

8 Place your buttons on top of the outline of the heart, and then fill in the heart with the rest of the buttons.

9 One by one, pick up the buttons, add a dab of glue to the back of the button and place back on the canvas. Press firmly for 10 seconds.

10 Let your canvas dry for one hour—more outdoor playtime!

11 Once the canvas is dry, have your an adult help you display it on your wall!

PIZZA BOX CANVAS ART

Pizza parties can now be fun art parties! Ever wonder what to do with those leftover pizza boxes? Turn them into a pizza box canvas and share your artistic skills (make sure to eat all the pizza first). This is the perfect project to learn the importance of recycling and reusing.

Age: 4+ with adult supervision

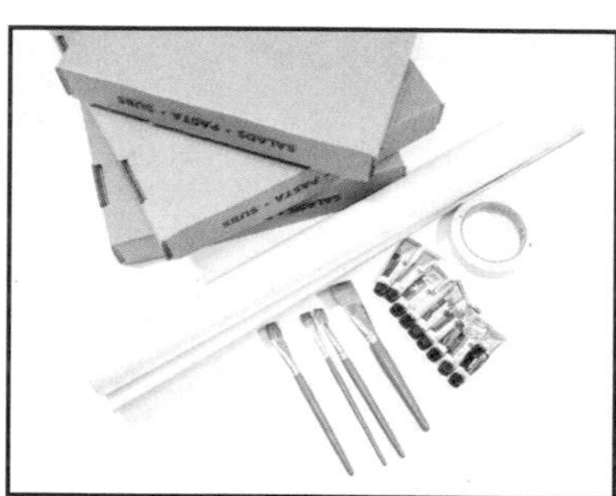

MATERIALS

- Medium pizza boxes
- Large poster paper sheets or flip chart paper
- Masking tape
- Paint set
- Paintbrush

DIRECTIONS

1 Have an adult help you wrap each pizza box with the poster paper or flip chart paper and secure the edges using masking tape.

2 Paint a picture on each canvas using the paint set and paintbrush.

3 Allow paint to dry.

4 Have an adult help you display your pictures in your room!

Tip: Come up with a story and paint each scene of the story on a separate canvas. Then, gather all your friends and family and tell the story that your canvas illustrates.

SALT ART

Salt art is the homemade version of sand art from the country fair. You can create endless fun designs and keep them on display in your room. This is the perfect project to experiment with mixing colors and making patterns. Remember—it is much healthier to play with salt than to eat it!

Age: 3+

MATERIALS

- 4 cups of salt
- (4) 1-gallon sealable bags
- 4 colors of food coloring
- 4 bowls
- Spoon
- Sealable glass jar
- 1 bamboo skewer

DIRECTIONS

1 Pour 1 cup of salt into the first sealable bag.

2 Add 2–3 drops of food coloring and seal the bag, making sure all the air is out.

3 Roll the bag and the salt between your hands, spreading the dye around.

4 Keep doing this until all the salt is colored.

5 Repeat steps 1–4 for the remaining colors.

6 Pour each bag of salt with the spoon into a bowl.

7 Start creating your art by laying the salt with the spoon in a glass jar.

8 Once you have the desired amount of layers, take your bamboo skewer and push it down along the sides of the jar to create artistic mixes of the colors.

9 Once you have your desired mix, screw the lid on and display on a shelf to admire.

WATERCOLOR ART: SALT AND CRAYON

Create the next Picasso or Van Gogh art masterpiece and let your creativity shine! Add texture to your painting with salt or send a secret message in this cool watercolor and white crayon art painting.

Age: 5+ with adult supervision

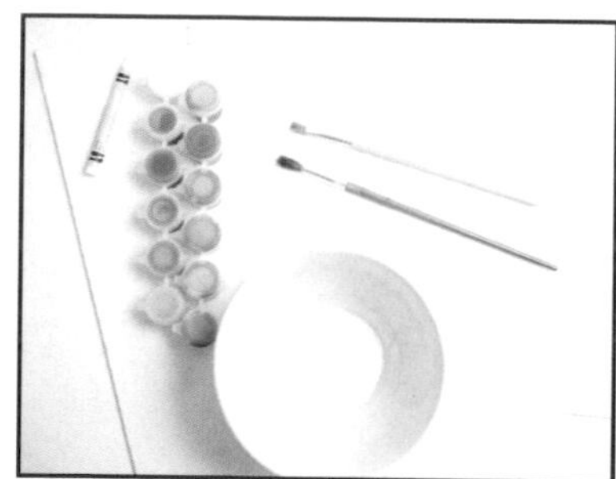

MATERIALS

- Cardstock
- White crayon
- Watercolor paper
- Watercolor paint
- Paintbrush
- Table salt

DIRECTIONS

Salt Design:

1 Using the watercolors, paint a design on a piece of watercolor paper.

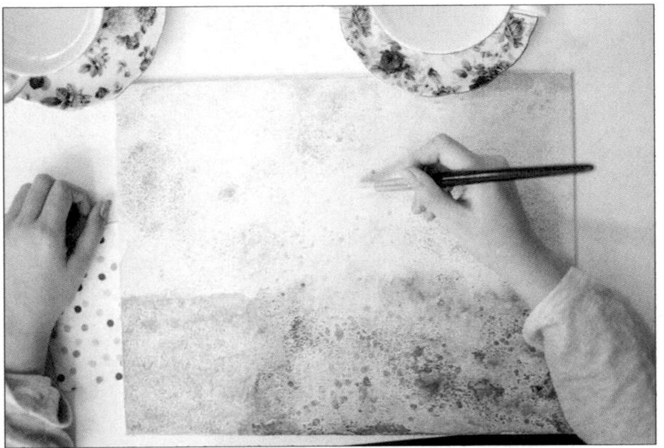

2 While the art is still very wet, sprinkle salt in the select areas. Place the salt inside of shapes or in areas you want to highlight.

3 Let the painting dry for 1 hour with the salt on it.

4 When the painting is completely dry, shake off the excess salt over the trash can.

5 Check out how the salt lightened the paint and slightly spread out the color.

6 Now that you see the cool things you can do with these two techniques, you can get even more creative with your designs.

DIRECTIONS

White Crayon Design:

1 Draw a shape on the cardstock using the white crayon and cut it out.

2 Take your shape and place it on your watercolor paper. Use the white crayon and trace around the outside of the shape you just cut out. Draw other pictures or shapes on the watercolor paper using the white crayon.

3 Using the watercolor paint and paintbrush, paint over the drawings you just made. Paint the entire paper with the watercolor paint.

4 Let your project dry for one hour and your secret art will be revealed.

5 Hang and decorate!

PAINTER'S TAPE ABSTRACT ART

Try your hand at abstract art. We have made it simple and easy to create a perfect work of art using painter's tape. You don't have to worry about painting within the lines or messing up your art work.

Age: 6+

MATERIALS

- Newspaper or parchment paper
- Canvas, any size
- Painter's tape
- 3–4 colors of acrylic paint
- Paintbrush

DIRECTIONS

1 Cover your work surface with newspapers or parchment paper.

2 Lay your canvas flat on the work surface.

3 Create a design using the painter's tape. Make sure you push down and seal the tape so it is really stuck.

4 Paint in between the tape marks using your acrylic paint and paintbrush.

5 Let the canvas dry for one hour.

6 Peel away the tape to reveal your beautiful abstract work of art.

HAND-STAMPED GREETING CARDS

Handwritten and designed cards are the perfect way to show your parents, friends and family you care. Create a unique design for them by making your own stamps. This is a one-of-a-kind card that they will not find anywhere else!

Age: 6+ with adult supervision

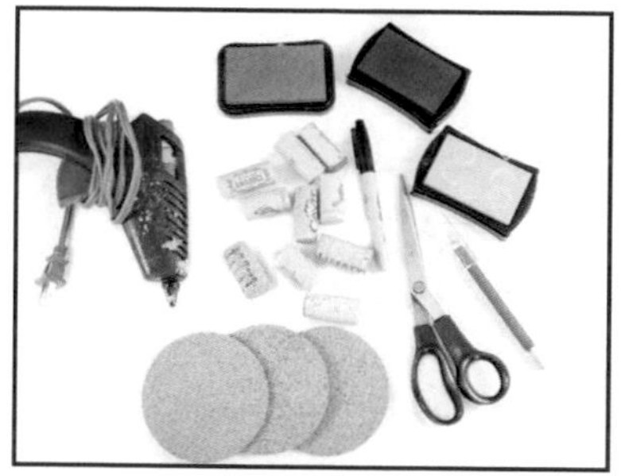

MATERIALS

- Black marker
- 3 round cork coasters
- X-Acto knife
- Scissors
- Hot glue gun
- 8–10 bottle corks
- White cardstock
- Ink pads in various colors
- Envelopes to fit the size of your cards (optional)

DIRECTIONS

1 Use the black marker to draw the letters H, E, L, L, O, I, U and a heart shape on the cork coasters.

2 Use the X-Acto knife and scissors to cut around all the letters and the heart. Trim off the excess cork coaster.

3 Using the hot glue gun, glue the cork letters and the heart to the ends of the bottle corks.

4 Using the scissors, cut the white cardstock sheets into 6 x 5-inch cards.

5 Fold the cards in half hamburger style to create a card.

6 Stamp each letter with a different color inkpad to make a colorful greeting card.

7 Use appropriately sized envelopes to complete your personalized note.

VEGETABLE-STAMPED TOTE BAG

Playing with your food has a whole new meaning with this project—Your parents will definitely not yell at you for doing it. Instead of letting them throw out dated vegetables, ask them to let you use them for this fun work of art!

Age: 6+

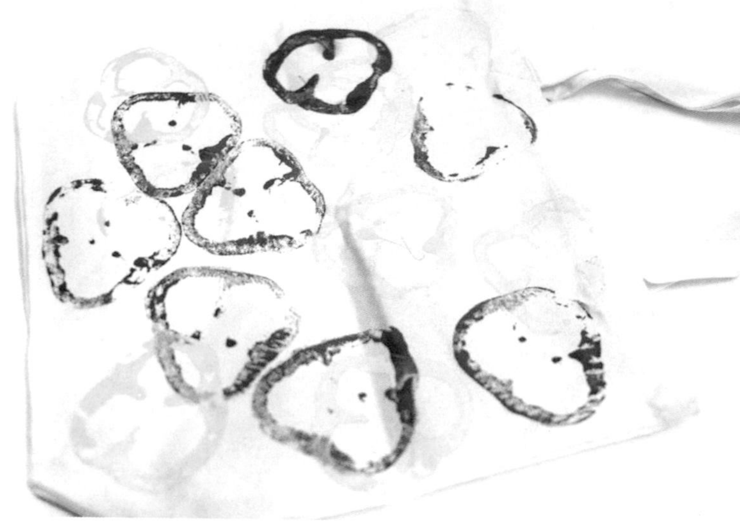

MATERIALS

- Parchment paper
- Tote bag
- Fabric Creations fabric paint
- 2 foam brushes
- Bell peppers cut in half and deseeded
- Various other fruits and vegetables (apples, carrots, etc.)
- White towel
- Iron

DIRECTIONS

1 Cover a work table with parchment paper. Place your tote bag in the middle.

2 Squeeze half-dollar-size amounts of fabric paint onto the parchment paper.

3 Use the foam brush to spread out the paint to a large enough area to stamp a bell pepper.

4 Press a cut bell pepper into the paint, pull it straight up and stamp it straight down on the tote bag. Hold it for three seconds and pull it straight up.

5 Repeat with multiple colors. Use a different bell pepper half for each color. Try using other fruits and vegetables like apples, artichokes, carrots, celery, and avocado.

6 Let your tote dry for one hour.

7 Have an adult put a white towel over your tote once it is dry and iron it on a medium setting to set the paint. Once you have ironed your tote, it can be washed in the washing machine.

DUCT TAPE TOTE BAG

Are you a budding fashionista? This easy duct tape tote bag is the perfect opportunity to try your hand at being a fashion designer. This simple project will teach coordination skills, design and how to closely follow instructions.

Age: 10+

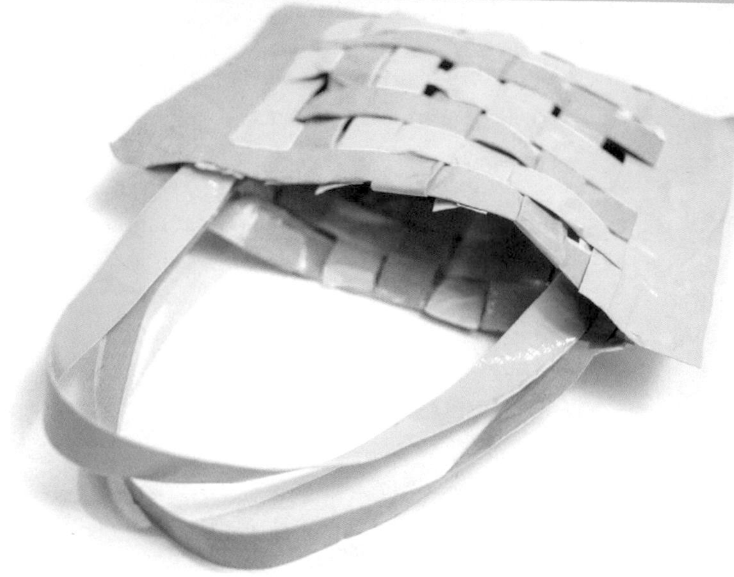

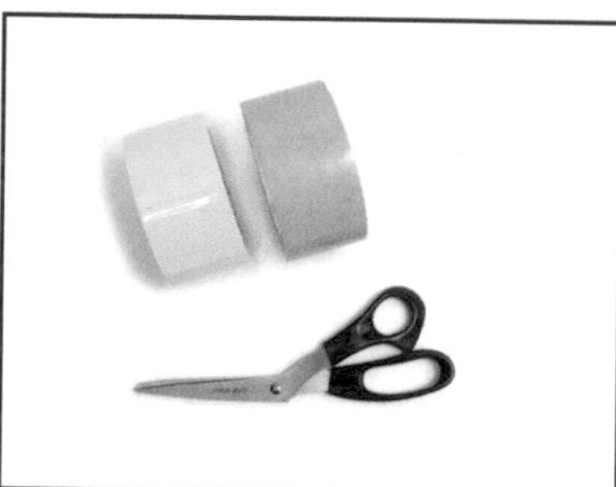

MATERIALS

- Ruler
- 2 different rolls of colored duct tape
- Scissors

DIRECTIONS

1 Measure one 16-inch strip of duct tape and fold it in half so the sticky sides stick together and the piece is still 16 inches long. Repeat three times.

2 Repeat step 1 four times with the second color of duct tape.

3 Measure one 12-inch strip of duct tape and fold it like you did in step one. The sticky sides will stick together and the strip will still be 12 inches long. Repeat six times with the same color of duct tape.

4 Repeat step 3 five times with the second color of duct tape.

5 On a flat surface lay the 16-inch strips of duct tape from steps 1 and 2 vertically, alternating colors.

6 Take each 12-inch strip you created in steps 3 and 4 and weave them horizontally through the 16-inch strips you laid out in step 5. Weave them by going over and under each of the 16-inch strips. Alternate the colors of the 12-inch strips.

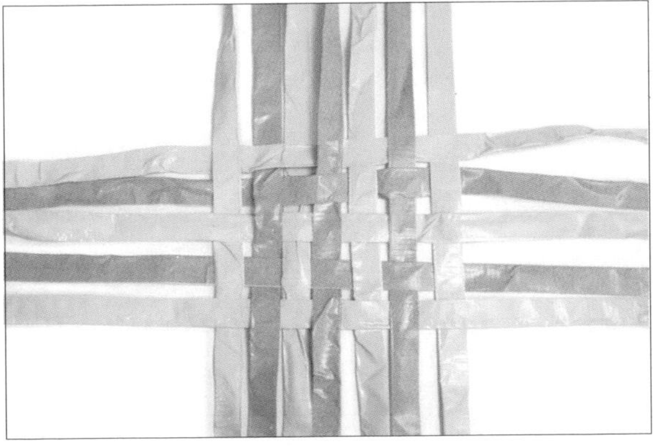

7 Fold the weaved strips in half.

8 Trim excess ends of duct tape so they are even on all sides.

9 Cut two 16-inch strip of duct tape and use them to seal the edges of the bag.

10 Cut one 16-inch strip of duct tape in each color and fold them in half like you did in step 1. The sticky sides should be sticking together. These will be the handles of your bag.

11 Using small pieces of duct tape, tape the straps to the inside of the bag.

12 Congratulations! You just created your first piece of custom-designed fashion!

TERRARIUM

Plants can be fun and a great way to show your parents you are responsible. Practice taking care of plants with a custom-made terrarium. Pick out a variety of funky-looking succulent plants and mini cacti to display in your plant creation.

Age: 8+

MATERIALS

- Pebbles
- Glass bowl
- Potting soil
- Succulents and cacti
- Sand

DIRECTIONS

1 Add a 1 to 2-inch layer of pebbles in the bottom of your bowl.

2 Add 3 inches of potting soil on top of the pebbles.

3 Add the plants.

4 Add a top layer of sand in the bowl to cover any of the potting soil still showing, making sure the plant roots are covered.

How to Take Care of Your Terrarium

Place your terrarium in a well-lit room. You will only need to water it once a week. Touch the soil and do not water until the soil is completely dry.

{ ART DECOR }

CHALKBOARD FRAME

Chalkboards are becoming more and more popular. They provide a great outlet to express your creativity, practice homework, draw a story or perfect your handwriting. The best part is that the chalkboard is reusable 100 times over!

Age: 4+ with adult supervision

MATERIALS

- Old newspapers or craft paper
- Wood-framed mirror
- Foam brush
- Chalkboard paint
- Acrylic brown paint
- Decorative tape
- Sticker alphabet letters
- Chalk or chalkboard markers

DIRECTIONS

1 Cover a flat surface with old newspapers or craft paper.

2 Remove the glass mirror from the frame, place it on a covered surface and use the foam brush to paint it with chalkboard paint.

3 Set the mirror aside and let it dry for 30 minutes.

4 While the painted mirror is drying, paint the wooden frame with acrylic paint.

5 Let the frame dry for 30 minutes. This is a perfect time to go outside and play or read a book!

6 Once the frame is dry, place a few pieces of decorative tape across the top panel of the frame and spell out your name with sticker letters on top of the decorative tape.

7 Insert the chalkboard-painted mirror into the center of the frame and reattach all back pieces. Use chalk or a chalk marker to start drawing on your new chalkboard.

8 Display in your room so you can create and recreate anytime!

Tip: Use a wet paper towel to dampen the board before writing on it. This technique will help the chalk or chalk marker wipe off easier.

TILE COASTERS

Make coasters with old tiles from one of your parent's renovation projects. Personalize them with your favorite patterns of decorative paper. If you want to get really crafty, you can use photographs of you and your friends and family instead of decorating paper. The creative freedom is in your hands. These also make a great gift for Mother's Day or Father's Day.

Age: 6+

MATERIALS

- 4 white square subway tiles
- Decorative paper
- Pencil
- Scissors
- 16 mini self-adhesive rubber stoppers
- Foam brush
- Mod Podge

DIRECTIONS

1 Place one of your tiles on the backside of the decorative paper and trace it with the pencil.

2 Use the scissors to cut it out.

3 Repeat steps 1–2 with the other three tiles.

4 Turn all four tiles over so the non-shiny sides are facing upward.

5 Stick one mini rubber stopper in each corner.

6 Flip tiles over so the shiny side is facing up.

7 Using your foam brush, spread a coat of Mod Podge evenly across the entire shiny side of the tile.

8 Lay one of the squares of decorative paper you cut out on top of the Mod Podge surface. Use your fingers to press down and smooth out the bubbles.

9 Let the tile dry for three minutes. While it is drying, complete steps 7–8 with the other three tiles.

10 Go back to your first tile and, using the foam brush, spread an even layer of Mod Podge over the top of the decorative paper. Use your fingers to smooth out any bubbles. Let it dry for three to five minutes.

11 While your first tile is drying, complete step 10 on the other three tiles.

12 Add two to three more coats of Mod Podge to each tile, waiting three minutes in between coats.

13 Let all the tiles dry for one hour before using them.

PAINTED BEAD BRACELET

It is never too early to start designing your own jewelry and accessories. Pick out your own colors and show off your creativity on your wrist with a homemade bracelet. Make one to match every outfit.

Age: 5+ with adult supervision

MATERIALS

- Scissors
- Ruler
- Elastic string
- Wooden beads
- Yarn
- Paper plate
- 4 acrylic paint colors

DIRECTIONS

1 Using the scissors and a ruler, measure and cut 8 inches of elastic string.

2 Tie a triple knot on one end of the elastic string.

3 Thread the beads and tie three knots to close in the beads.

4 Using the scissors and ruler, cut and measure 8 inches of yarn.

5 Squeeze several drops of one paint color onto the paper plate.

6 Twist the yarn on each index finger and dip the middle of the yarn in one paint color.

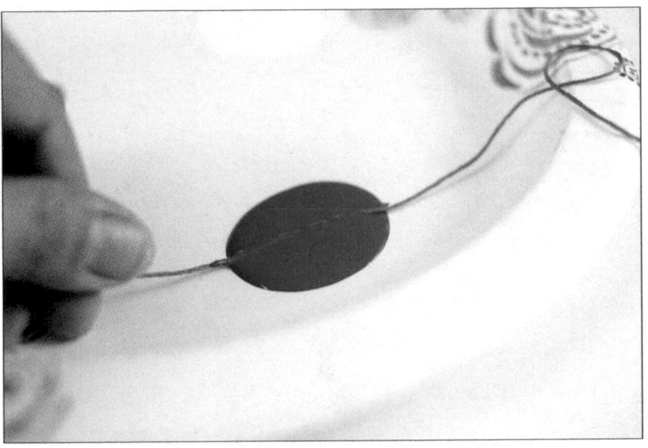

7 Wrap the paint-covered yarn around the beads. Switch up the pattern and direction of the lines.

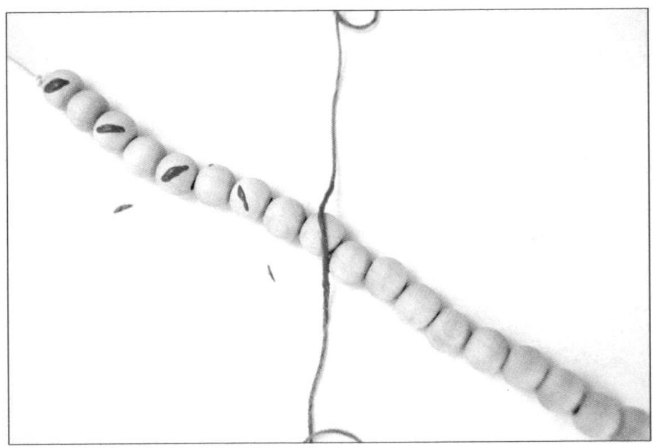

8 Continue steps 4–7 with each paint color until you have a mixed color pattern.

9 Let the paint dry for 30 minutes.

10 Tie the bracelet together and cut off the excess elastic string.

11 Have fun showing off your personalized fashion and work of art!

DREAM CATCHER

Dream catchers were created by Native Americans to filter out bad dreams and only allow good thoughts to enter your mind each night. It's easy to make your own dream catcher and protective charm. Hang this by your bed and you are sure to have sweet dreams.

Age: 10+

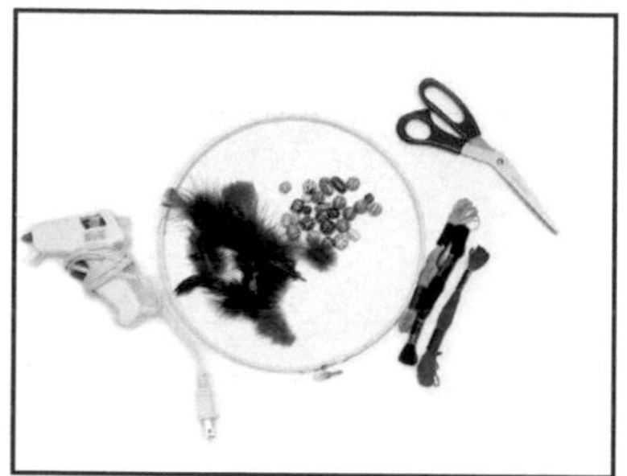

MATERIALS

- Cotton embroidery thread in various colors
- Wooden embroidery hoop
- Scissors
- Beads
- School glue
- Feathers

DIRECTIONS

1 Tie a piece of cotton embroidery thread to the top of the embroidery hoop using several knots.

2 Stretch the embroidery thread across the hoop to the opposite side and wrap around, down and back to the top.

3 Change your angle slightly and continue the same back and forth movement around the entire hoop, creating a spider web.

4 After you create a spider web across the entire hoop, tie off the end of the string with two knots.

5 Repeat steps 1–4 for additional colors.

6 Tie three 12-inch strings 1 inch apart at the bottom of the hoop.

7 String beads to each hanging string, then tie a knot below the beads to keep them on the string.

8 Glue a feather to the end of each hanging string.

9 Let it dry and hang above your bed for protection. Get ready to have lots of really fun and happy dreams!

RECYCLED CRAYON MOLDS

Don't let broken and dull crayons make you sad. You now can recycle them into fun shapes and cool mixed colors. Try this craft with all kinds of different molds!

Age: 5+ with adult supervision

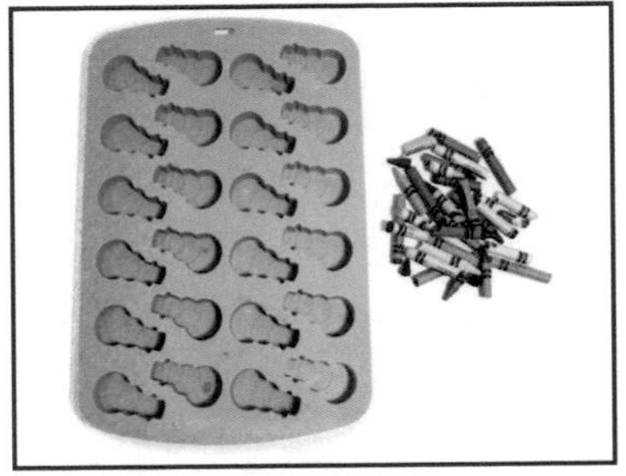

MATERIALS

- Broken crayons
- Silicon mold
- Baking tray

DIRECTIONS

1 Have an adult preheat the oven to 200°F.

2 Gather up all of your broken crayons.

3 Have an adult help you remove all the papers.

4 Place the silicon mold on a baking tray.

5 Fill the silicon mold with the broken crayons. Mix up the colors to get a rainbow look.

6 Have an adult put the pan in the oven, and set the timer for 10 minutes.

7 Have an adult remove the pan after 10 minutes if the crayons are fully melted. If not, bake for another few minutes, and check on them frequently.

8 Set the crayons out until they are hard (approximately 15 minutes).

9 Once they are hard, pop them out of the silicon mold and start coloring!

NO-SEW KITCHEN APRON

Cooking can be really messy. Keep your clothes clean with a pretty apron. Patterned aprons add the right amount of fun for your first cooking experience! This apron is a no-sew, so it is super easy with just a little help from an adult. This is a great project to learn how to follow instructions and create your own unique design.

Age: 7+ with adult supervision

MATERIALS

- Measuring tape
- Shearing scissors
- ½ yard of fabric
- Iron
- Clear fabric glue
- Lace trim
- 2-inch-wide twill ribbon

DIRECTIONS

1 Have an adult measure around your waist with the measuring tape and divide that number in half. This number will be the width of your apron.

2 Next, measure the length from your waist to your knee.

3 Take your length and width measurements and cut out a rectangle of that size from the fabric. For example, if your width is 10 inches and your length is 12 inches, then the rectangle shape you cut out will be 10 x 12 inches in size.

4 Fold over about 1 inch on the long sides of the rectangle, and have an adult iron them down.

5 Using the fabric glue, dab dots inside the fold and press down to seal the hem.

6 Whatever the distance around your waist, double that number to get the total length for the ribbon and the lace trim. Use the scissors to cut the ribbon and lace.

7 After you cut the ribbon length, find the center and glue that piece to the center of the top edge of the fabric.

8 Lightly dab glue to the edge of the fabric to attach the ribbon. There should be plenty of ribbon that hangs off the edges to wrap around your waist.

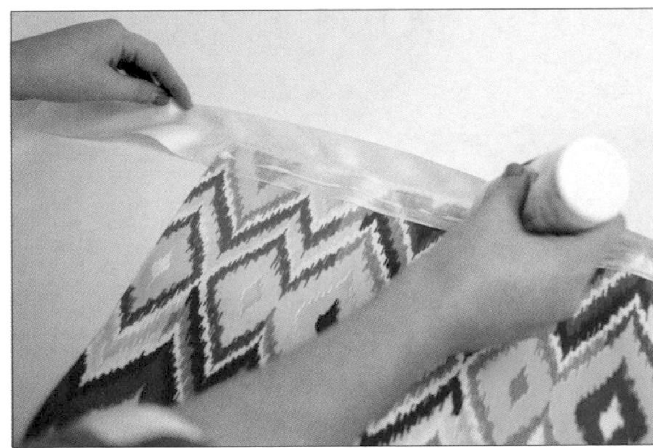

9 Repeat steps 8 9 with the lace trim on the other end (bottom) of your apron.

10 Allow the apron to dry for 24 hours before using. Wait 7 days before washing.

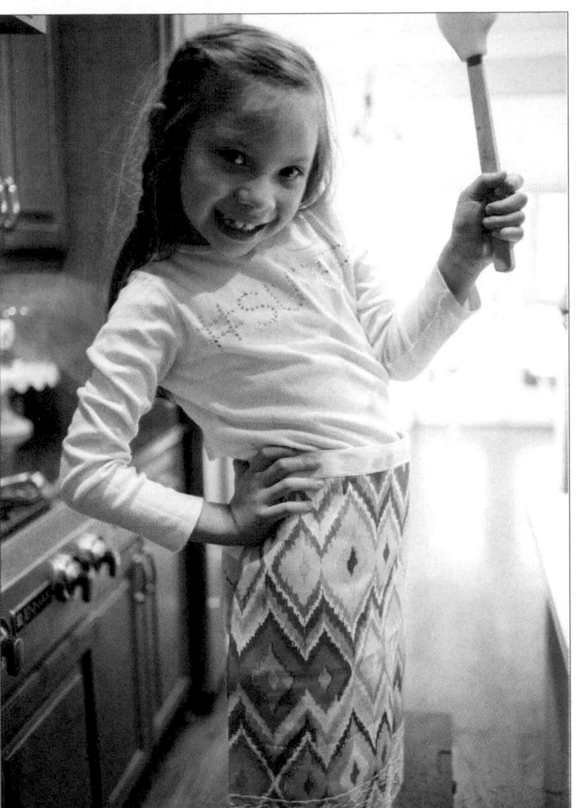

NO-SEW BURLAP PLACE SETTING

Make dinnertime more exciting with creative place settings, such as handmade place mats and drink wraps. These add a special touch to an everyday meal, a special birthday celebration or an outdoor picnic. Make individual place settings for everyone in the family!

Age: 9+

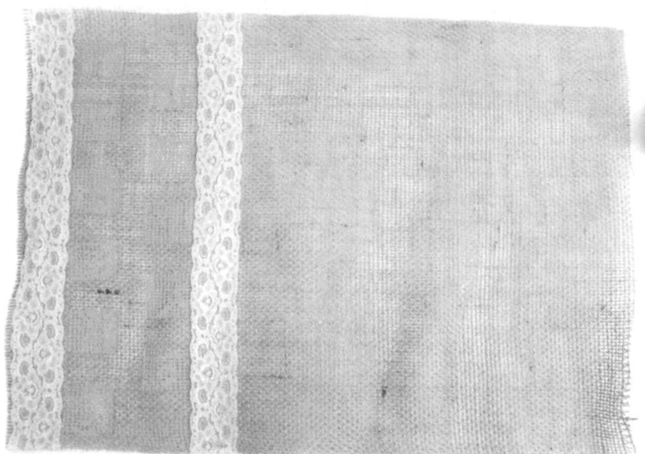

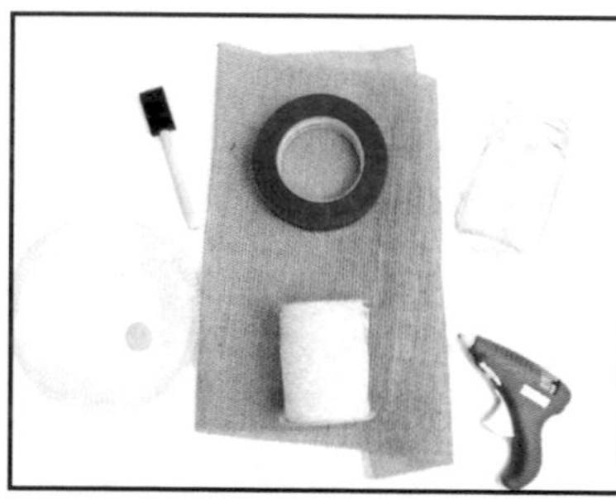

MATERIALS

- 12-inch wide burlap roll
- Ruler
- Marker
- Scissors
- Painter's tape or stencils
- Acrylic paint
- Foam brush
- Lace or decorative ribbon
- Hot glue gun
- Mason jar

DIRECTIONS

Burlap Place Mat:

1 Spread out the burlap roll and measure 18 inches in length with your ruler. Draw a straight line at 18 inches with a marker.

2 Use your scissors to cut along the marker line you just drew. Your placemat should be 12 x 18 inches.

3 Use painter's tape and/or stencils to make a creative design as an outline for painting. If you are using stencils, use the painter's tape to tape them down.

4 Paint your design using the acrylic paint and foam brush. Leave the stencil or painter's tape in place and let dry for 30 minutes.

5 If you want to add lace or decorative ribbon, grab an adult and have them help you use the hot glue gun to secure the ribbon.

Drink Wrap:

1 Roll out your burlap and use your ruler to measure and draw a 4 x 7-inch rectangle (measured to fit a standard mason jar).

2 Use the scissors to cut out the rectangle you just drew.

3 Use painter's tape and/or stencils to make a creative design as an outline for painting. If you are using stencils, use the painter's tape to tape them down.

4 Paint your design using the acrylic paint and foam brush. Leave the stencil or painter's tape in place and let dry for 30 minutes.

5 If you want to add lace or decorative ribbon, grab an adult and have them help you use the hot glue gun to secure the ribbon.

6 Once your wrap is dry, wrap it around the jar tightly with just enough room to slip it on and off. Secure the wrap by hot gluing (with an adult's help) the ends together tight enough to stay on the jar but loose enough to slip on and off. Trim extra burlap off the ends after securing.

7 Make a set for everyone in your family! When it comes time to clean, hand wash only by using paper towels or a rag to wipe clean.

RECIPE BOOK

Want to play chef in the kitchen? Every chef needs a recipe book to store all the new recipes they learn. This fun activity allows you to create and decorate your own recipe book using a stamp, ink pad and notebook rings.

Age: 10+

MATERIALS

- Scissors
- 1 sheet of 12 x 12-inch decorative scrapbook paper
- White cardstock paper, cut into 4 x 6-inch rectangles
- Hole puncher
- Black marker or recipe card stamp and black ink pad
- 2 notebook rings
- 1 sheet of 12 x 12-inch decorative scrapbook paper in a different design
- Glue stick

DIRECTIONS

1 Using the scissors, cut the decorative scrapbook paper in half.

2 Fold the scrapbook paper into a 4 x 6-inch card, gluing the remaining paper on the back. This is the cover of the recipe book. Do this to the other half sheet of scrapbook paper to make a back cover.

3 Use the hole puncher to punch two holes at the top of the cover and on all of the white 4 x 6-inch cardstock.

4 Stamp the recipe stamp on the white cardstock. If you do not have a recipe stamp use a black marker to write the world recipe at the top of the paper and draw lines across the paper.

5 Let the ink dry for at least 5 minutes.

6 Place the back cover with the inside facing up, add the cardstock recipe cards and top with the cover. Line up the holes and assemble the covers and recipe cards by looping them through the notebook rings.

7 Use the remaining scrapbook paper and cut out any designs or letters. Stick them with the glue to decorate the book cover.

8 Now that you have a recipe book, you need to fill it with recipes. Start by using the easy recipes in this book, and then ask your parents to teach you a few more!

IN THE KITCHEN

CHOCOLATE PRETZEL POPCORN

Pop, pop, pop goes the popcorn! Movie night just got a lot better! Surprise your friends with a tasty custom popcorn recipe. Get creative with the toppings you add for a new treat every time.

Age: 7+ with adult supervision

MATERIALS

- 6 cups popped popcorn
- Large mixing bowl
- 5 ounces milk chocolate chips
- Microwave-safe bowl
- Pot holder
- Spatula
- 1 cup mini marshmallows
- 1 cup crushed pretzels
- Sprinkles
- Spoon

DIRECTIONS

1 Pour popcorn into the bowl.

2 Put the chocolate chips in a microwave-safe bowl and microwave 30 seconds at a time. After each 30 seconds, remove the bowl using a pot holder and stir the chocolate with a spatula. Continue to microwave in 30-second increments until the chocolate is completely melted and smooth.

3 Drizzle the melted chocolate into the large bowl with the popcorn.

4 Add marshmallows and crushed pretzels to the popcorn bowl.

5 Use the mixing spatula to mix the popcorn and evenly distribute the chocolate, marshmallow and pretzel.

6 Shake sprinkles over the mixture and stir.

7 Let the chocolate in the popcorn harden for 15 minutes.

8 Our favorite way to enjoy our chocolaty popcorn creation is in a homemade chocolate bowl (see page 104)!

CHOCOLATE BOWLS

I often say everything tastes better with chocolate. Why not enjoy your favorite snack out of a chocolate bowl? The best part is that it is super easy, and you can eat your bowl at the end!

Age: 10+

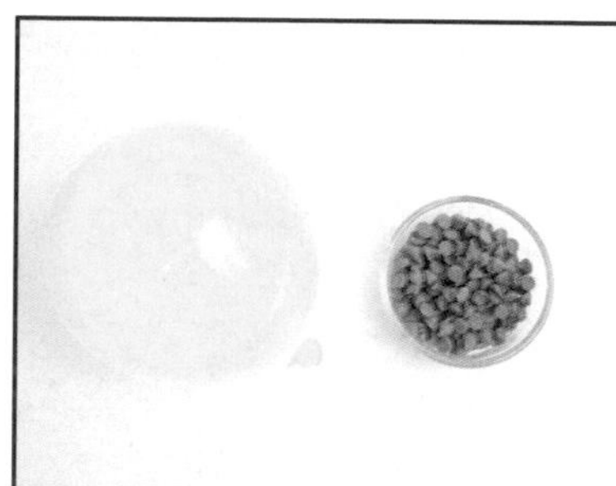

MATERIALS

- 4 standard balloons
- Soap and water
- (1) 10-ounce package of milk chocolate chips
- Large microwave-safe bowl
- Pot holder
- Spoon
- Parchment paper
- Scissors

DIRECTIONS

1 Blow up the balloons to a third of their full size and tie them shut. Wash the outside of the balloons with soap and water and dry thoroughly. Set them aside for the next step.

2 Pour chocolate chips into a large microwave-safe bowl.

3 Microwave the chocolate for 30 seconds at a time. After each 30 seconds, remove the bowl using a pot holder and stir the chocolate with a spoon. Continue to microwave in 30-second increments until the chocolate is completely melted and smooth.

4 Line the counter or a table with parchment paper.

5 Once the chocolate is melted, grab the balloons and, one at a time, hold the balloon by the knot and dip it into the chocolate, pushing it down until the chocolate is halfway up the balloon. Repeat two more times to create a thick covering of chocolate.

6 Place the balloon with the chocolate part touching the parchment paper.

7 Repeat steps 5–6 for the other three balloons.

8 Let the chocolate balloons dry for at least one hour or until the chocolate has fully hardened.

9 Once the chocolate has hardened, pop the balloons by cutting a small hole by the knot with scissors.

10 Carefully peel the balloon out of the chocolate bowl.

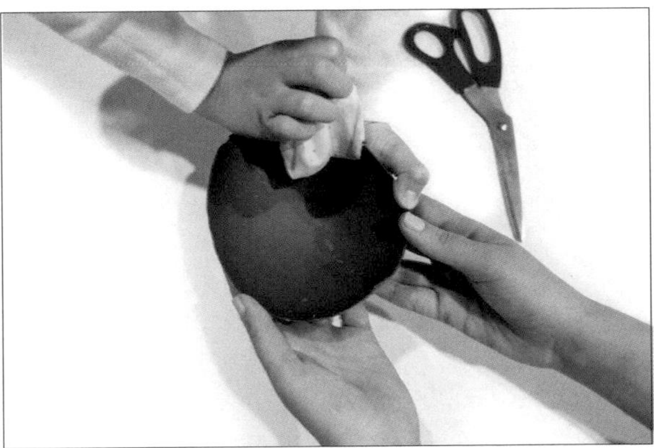

11 Enjoy your favorite snack in the chocolate bowl—our favorite is Chocolate Pretzel Popcorn (page 102).

ORGANIC FRUIT JUICE CANDY POPS

Ice pops can be full of sugar and really unhealthy. Organic and sugar-free pops are a great treat to share with friends on a hot sunny day!

Age: 2+ with adult supervision

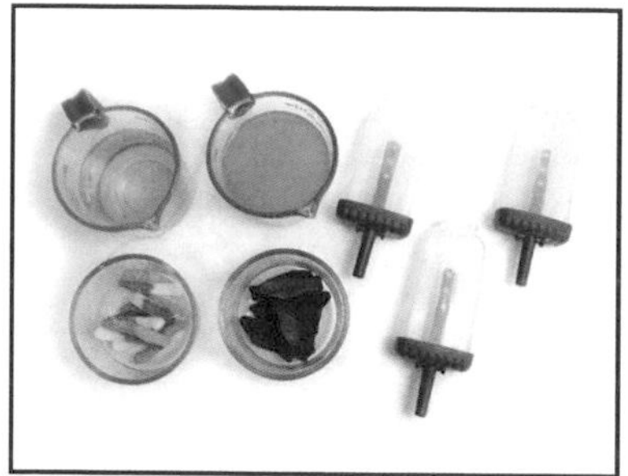

MATERIALS

- Sugar-free gummy candy
- Popsicle molds
- Organic sugar-free lemonade and sugar-free tangerine juice

DIRECTIONS

1 Put 2–3 pieces of gummy candy in each Popsicle holder.

2 Fill each Popsicle holder with juice and place the stick top on.

3 Freeze for three to four hours.

4 When you are ready to enjoy the pops, remove from the freezer and run the outside of the pops holder under warm water for 20 seconds to loosen the Popsicle.

NO-BAKE ICE CREAM CAKE

I scream, you scream, we all scream for ICE CREAM! Every day is an occasion for this favorite treat. This easy, no-bake ice cream cake is the perfect recipe for you to experiment with in the kitchen. Add the recipe to your homemade recipe book and make sure to celebrate this perfectly delicious cake with your friends and family.

Age: 5+ with adult supervision

MATERIALS

- 2 half-gallon containers of ice cream
- 9 x 13-inch pan
- Spatula
- 1 box of Oreo cookies
- Big spoon
- 1 bottle of Magic Shell topping
- 2 tablespoons hot fudge
- 1 tub of Cool Whip
- Sprinkles

DIRECTIONS

1 Take the first half-gallon container of ice cream out of the freezer and allow to soften for about 15 minutes.

2 Take the softened ice cream and spread it out in the pan with a spatula.

3 Put the pan in the freezer for one hour.

4 While the pan is in the freezer, remove the white filling from the Oreo cookies, putting the shells in a bowl.

5 Crush the Oreo shells with a big spoon.

6 Heat up the Magic Shell in the microwave per the instructions on the bottle.

7 Add the entire bottle to the cookie crumbs and mix with the spoon.

8 Add the hot fudge to the chocolate cookie crumb mixture, and mix with the spoon.

9 Remove the pan from freezer and spread the crumb mixture evenly over the ice cream.

10 Put the pan back in the freezer for 30 minutes.

11 When you return the pan to the freezer, remove the second half-gallon container of ice cream from the freezer and allow to soften for about 15 minutes.

12 When the ice cream in the freezer has hardened, take it out and spread the second half-gallon container of ice cream on top of the cookie mixture. Freeze for one hour.

13 Spread a layer of Cool Whip as an icing layer on top of the ice cream cake and decorate with sprinkles.

TWO-INGREDIENT FRUIT ROLL-UPS

All-natural snacks are way healthier than the ones you buy in stores. They taste even better when you and your parents make them together. This recipe uses strawberries, but you can experiment with different fruits or combinations of fruits!

Age: 6+ with adult supervision

MATERIALS

- ½ cup strawberries, washed and hulled
- Blender
- ½ tablespoon all-natural honey
- Parchment paper
- Baking pan
- Spoon
- Scissors
- Plastic bag

DIRECTIONS

1 Preheat the oven to 175°F.

2 Pour strawberries in the blender and add honey.

3 Blend until the mixture has a liquid consistency.

4 Spread parchment paper out on the baking pan.

5 Pour mixture onto the parchment paper and spread evenly with a spoon.

6 Bake in the oven for two hours or until the mixture has dried.

7 Remove from the oven and let the fruit snack cool for one hour.

8 Use your scissors to cut the fruit snacks into strips. Cut through the parchment paper and fruit snacks.

9 Roll them up and store in a plastic bag. They will stay fresh for two weeks if stored in an airtight container.

GOOPY GOO

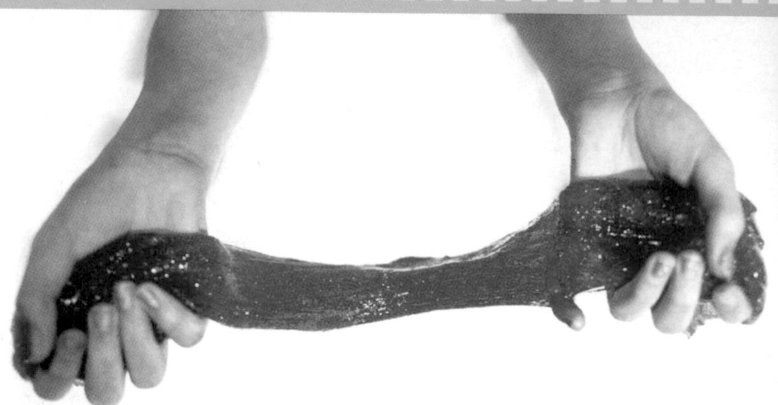

Goopy Goo sounds messy but it's actually pretty clean and will provide lots of entertainment and excitement. Discover the art of science with this simple recipe that goes from a liquid to a gooey formed blob because of the way the ingredients interact with one another! (It doesn't smell bad.)

Age: 6+ with adult supervision

MATERIALS

- 5-fl-oz (147-ml) container clear school glue
- 2 large mixing bowls
- Water
- Spoon
- Food coloring
- Silver glitter
- Large microwave-safe bowl
- Pot holder
- ½ cup hot water
- ½ teaspoon Borax

DIRECTIONS

1 Pour the bottle of glue in a large bowl. Fill the empty glue bottle to the top with water and dump it in the bowl of glue. Use a spoon to mix thoroughly.

2 Add three to four drops of food coloring and mix with the spoon.

3 Sprinkle glitter into the mix and stir well.

4 Heat up water in a microwave-safe bowl for 30–45 seconds. Remove from microwave using a pot holder.

5 Pour the ½ cup of hot water into the second large bowl.

6 Add the Borax to the hot water and mix until completely dissolved.

7 Add the Borax mixture to the bowl with the glue, stir, and watch the magic happen.

8 Keep mixing until the Goopy Goo is no longer liquid but more like a slime.

9 Have hours of fun with this safe goo!

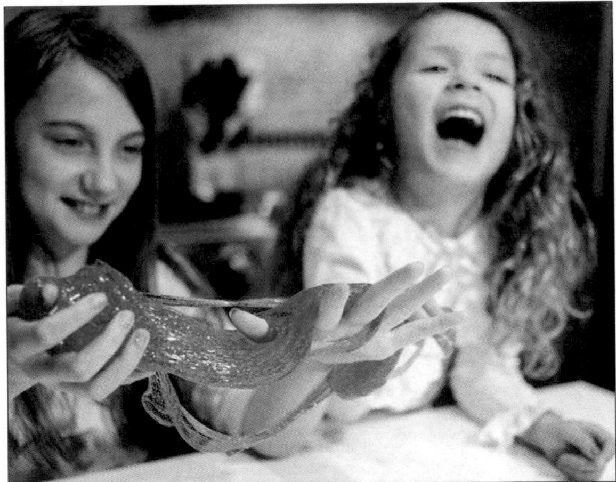

FLAVORED LIP BALM

Not only can you drink Kool-Aid, but you can make fun and tasty lip balms with it! Kool-Aid has so many great flavors and colors to choose from, so you can make one to match every outfit.

Age: 7+

MATERIALS

- Parchment paper
- 2 tablespoons coconut oil
- Microwave-safe bowl
- 2 spoons
- ½ packet of Kool-Aid
- Mixing bowl
- 2 tablespoons water
- 1 tablespoon sugar
- Whisk
- 10 small clear cosmetic containers

DIRECTIONS

1 Cover a clean, flat surface with parchment paper.

2 Put the coconut oil in a microwave-safe bowl and microwave for eight seconds to soften. Remove from the microwave and stir with a spoon.

3 Pour the Kool-Aid in the mixing bowl. Add the water and sugar. Stir until sugar is dissolved.

4 Add the Kool-Aid mixture to the coconut oil. Whip with a whisk until the mixture is completely smooth.

5 Use a small spoon to scoop mixture into cosmetic containers.

6 Place uncovered containers in the refrigerator for 10 minutes to allow the oil to regain a solid form. Remove from the refrigerator, replace the caps of the containers and they are ready to use or give away as gifts.

7 Add a sticker to the top to personalize your creation.

FOOD COLOR TIE-DYE SHIRT

Like bell bottoms (ask your grandparents) and flashy shirts, tie dye is still popular for all ages. Tie dye everything from your clothes to your sheets. This easy technique can be replicated on all types of cloth materials.

Age: 5+

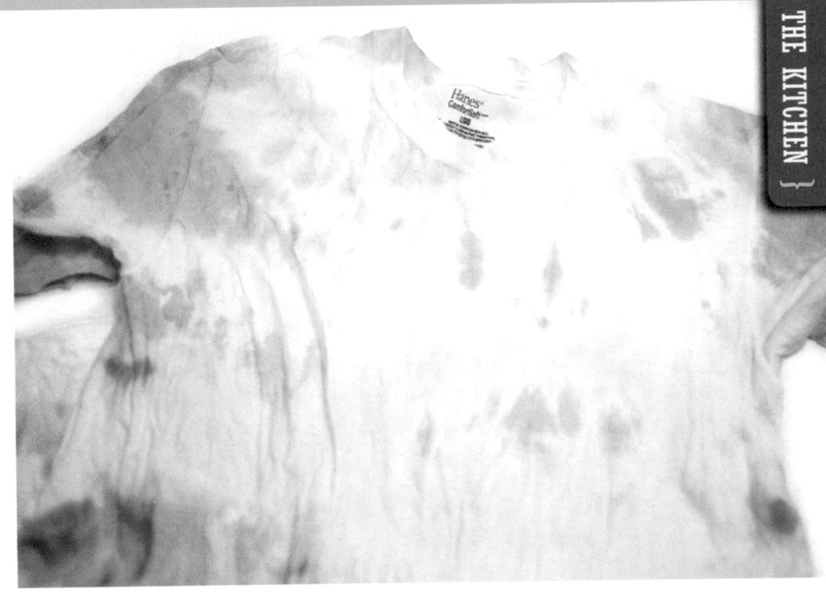

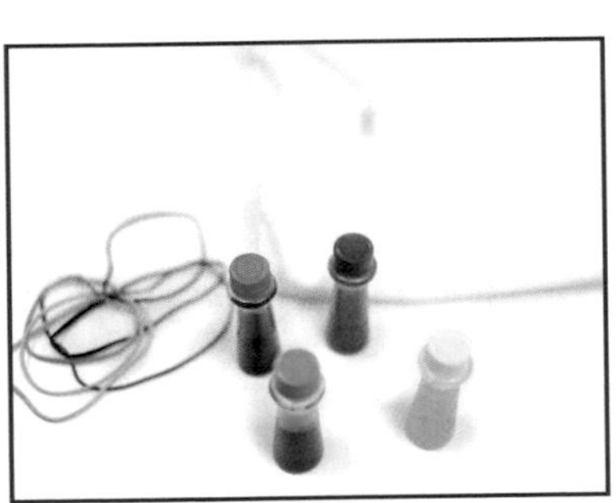

MATERIALS

- Parchment paper
- 1 prewashed white youth T-shirt
- Rubber bands
- 8 cups water
- 4 deep bowls
- Pink, blue, green, and yellow pastel food coloring
- 4 plastic spoons

DIRECTIONS

1 Spread parchment paper over the countertop or table you are working on.

2 Lay T-shirt flat and then gather it up by scrunching it into a roll.

3 Secure a rubber band around the T-shirt every 4 inches.

4 Twist the T-shirt around, then fold and secure in various places with a rubber band.

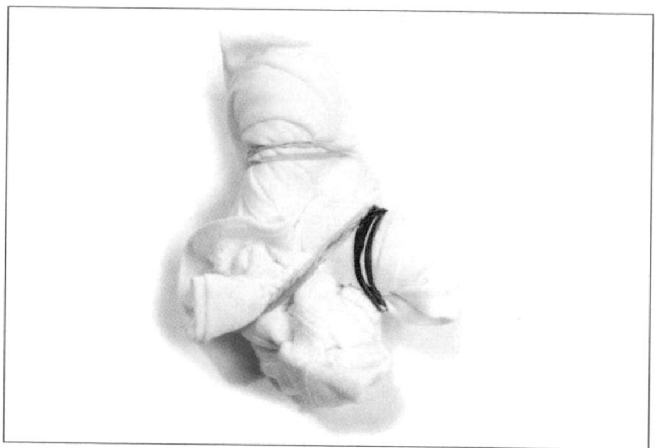

5 Add 2 cups of water to each of the four deep bowls.

6 Add 3 drops of yellow food coloring to one bowl. Repeat with the other colors and bowls.

7 Stir each bowl with a separate plastic spoon until the food coloring is thoroughly mixed.

8 Dip various parts of the T-shirt in each food coloring bowl. Overlap yellow and pink to make orange. Pink and blue will make purple.

9 Set your T-shirt on the parchment paper and let it dry for 24 hours.

10 Once it is dry, remove the rubber bands (save them for another project) and shake out the T-shirt to see your creative tie-dye design.

11 Throw the shirt in the dryer and dry on a high heat setting for 15–20 minutes to set the dye. After this, you can wash normally.

PAPER LUNCH BAG DECORATING

Brown paper bags are so dull! Lunchtime can be much more fun with a creative bag. Grab a few craft supplies and customize your lunch bags, and you will never get your lunch mixed up again!

Age: 5+

MATERIALS

- Scissors
- Construction paper
- Brown paper bags
- Glue stick
- Washi tape
- Pom-poms
- Googly eyes
- Pipe cleaners
- School glue
- Block stamps
- Ink pad

DIRECTIONS

Flower Design:

1 With scissors, carefully cut out flower petals from the construction paper. You may need about eight or nine petals, depending on how big you want your flower to be.

2 Next, cut out a circle for the center of the flower with a different colored construction paper.

3 Arrange the petals in a circular shape on the paper bag and glue them down with a glue stick. Then, glue the large circle down in the center of the petals.

4 Using washi tape, make a stem coming out from the flower to the bottom of the bag.

Tape Design:

1 Take your favorite color washi tape and make your own design on your bag.

2 Try your hand at stripes or diagonal lines.

3 Make sure to press the tape down firmly with your hand.

Dapper Wise Guy Design:

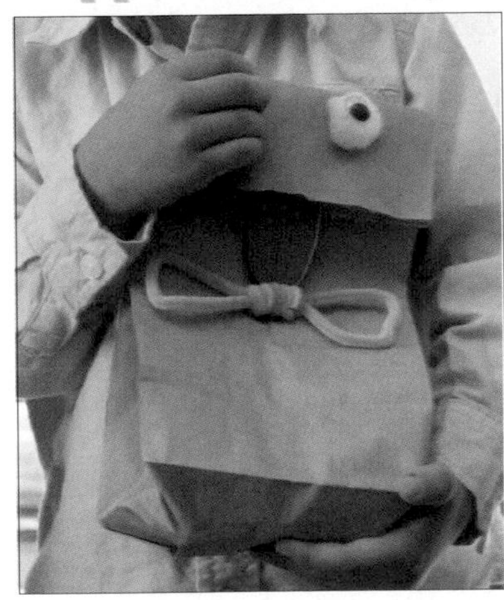

1 Fold the top of the bag over about 2 inches.

2 With red construction paper, cut out a U-shaped piece about 2 inches long.

3 Using the glue stick, glue that to the inside edge of the bag lining.

4 With the top of the bag still folded downward, take two pom-poms and glue them to the folded piece to create the eyes.

5 Use the school glue to glue googly eyes to the pom-poms.

6 Take one pipe cleaner and bend it to create the shape of a rectangle. Then, with a second pipe cleaner, wrap it around the center of the long sides of the rectangle to create a bow tie.

7 Glue the box tie to the lower half of the bag, below the tongue.

8 Allow bag to dry for 30–45 minutes.

Stamp Design:

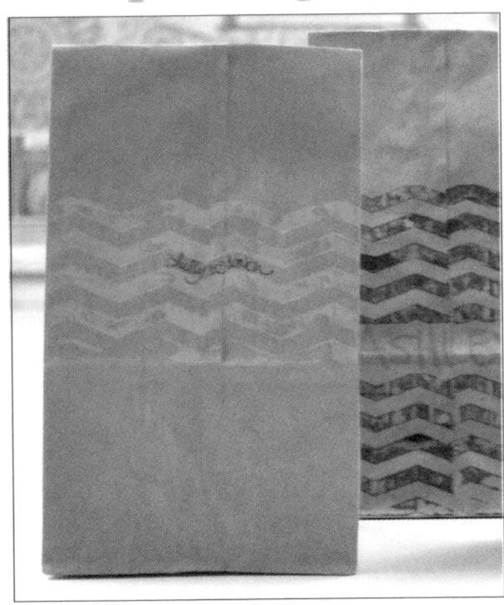

1 Lay your bag flat on a covered surface.

2 Pick your favorite stamps and color ink pads.

3 Press the stamp pad into the ink pad, then pick up and press onto the bag. Pick up and repeat.

BIRD FEEDER

Bird watching can be a terrific opportunity to enjoy nature. Attract beautiful birds to your yard with a hanging homemade bird feeder. If you have younger siblings, get them to help you with this fun craft!

Age: 10+

MATERIALS

- Parchment paper
- (2) 12-inch wooden dowels
- (3) 3 to 4-inch decorative wooden balls (find these at the craft store in the decorating section)
- 18-inch piece of string
- 2 spoons
- (1) 16-ounce jar of creamy peanut butter
- 1 cup bird seed

DIRECTIONS

1 This is a great project to do outdoors or in the kitchen. Just make sure your surface is covered with parchment paper to avoid a mess with sticky peanut butter.

2 Take one of the wooden dowels and feed it through the center of the three balls, leaving 1–2 inches on one end.

3 Take the other wooden dowel and feed it through the center of the end ball so the exposed dowel is centered on each side of the ball. It will look like a "T" shape.

4 Tie the string to each end of the horizontal dowel. Tie the remaining string to the top end of the vertical dowel, making a loop to hang.

5 Using your first spoon, spread peanut butter on each ball to completely cover.

6 Next, sprinkle bird seeds over each ball with the second spoon. Make sure to cover the entire ball with bird seed.

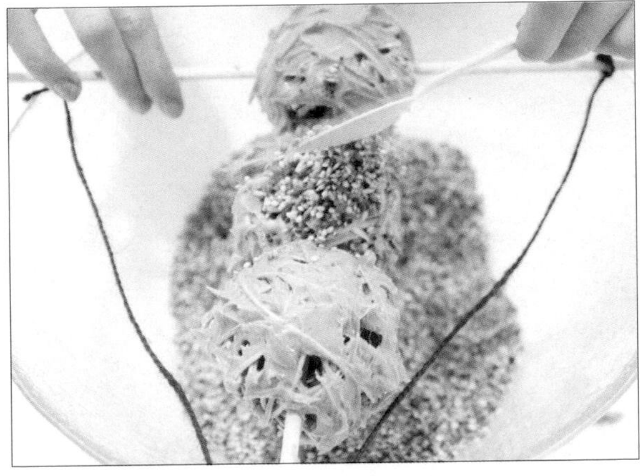

7 Your bird feeder is officially done! Grab your parents and ask them to help you hang it outside on a tree or near a window so you can watch the birds enjoying their lunch.

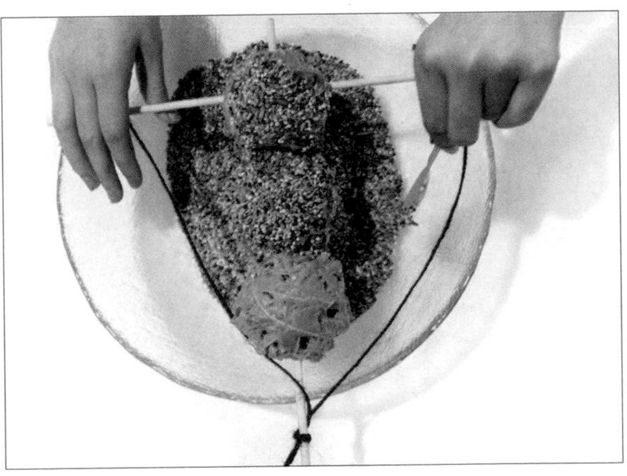

8 You can continue to refill the bird feeder with peanut butter and bird seed as it empties. This is the perfect craft to provide many months of enjoyment!

DOG COLLAR BOW TIE

Your pups deserve some crafty attention and creative inspiration. Have the best-dressed pooch in the neighborhood by dressing up his/her collar with a custom bow tie that easily slides on and off. Pick a fabric that matches your favorite outfit or a special occasion. Your pup will love the extra attention.

Age: 10+

MATERIALS

- Scissors
- Ruler
- 1 square foot of fabric
- Hot glue gun

DIRECTIONS

1 Using your scissors and a ruler, measure and cut a 7 x 4-inch piece of fabric.

2 Fold the fabric in half and hot glue the opening ends together.

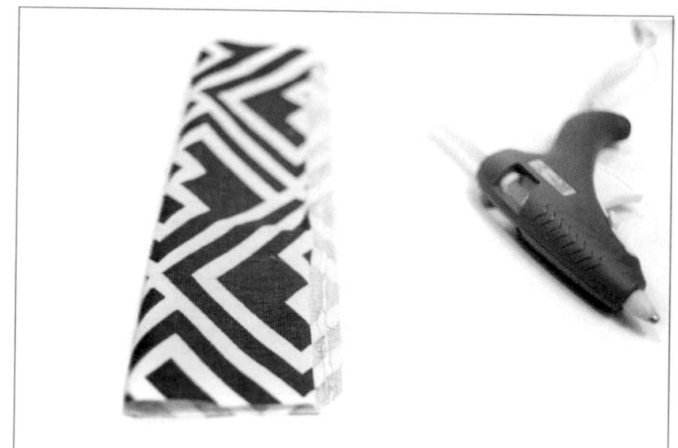

3 Shift the fabric so that the seam is on the back and is positioned in the middle.

4 Fold the piece of fabric in half so that the back fold is on the inside.

5 Hot glue the ends together.

6 Shift the fabric again so that the seam is on the back and is positioned in the middle.

7 Pinch and glue the bow together in the middle.

8 Using your ruler and scissors, measure and cut a second piece of fabric that is 3 × 1 inch.

9 Fold the 3 x 1-inch fabric in half and hot glue the opening ends together. Shift the fabric so that the seam is on the back and is positioned in the middle.

10 On the back of the bow, glue the 3 x 1-inch piece all around the middle, pinching in the bow tie as you wrap and tighten.

11 Tuck the remaining strip in the back to make a loop for the dog collar.

12 Let the glue dry.

13 Insert a dog collar through the loop.

14 Your pup will now be the most fashionably four-legged trendsetter on the block!

OLD T-SHIRT DOG TOY

If your dogs are like ours, they love to tear every toy apart. We finally found a toy that will withstand playtime and is great for tug-of-war. Grab a few of your old T-shirts—don't wash them because your dog will love the toy even more if it has your scent. Your pup is going to love this indestructible toy!

Age: 5+

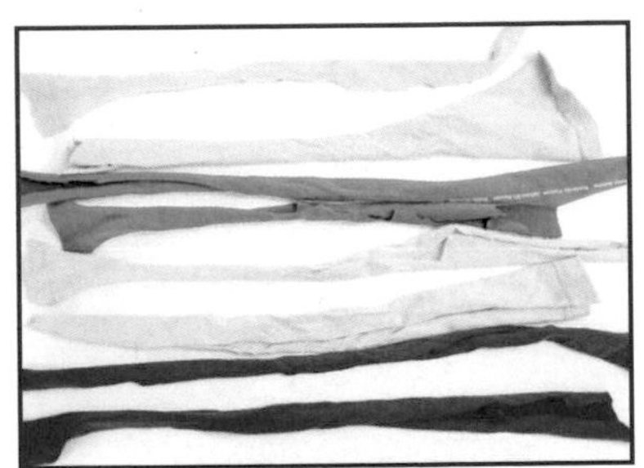

MATERIALS

- 3 old T-shirts you can cut up
- Scissors
- Ruler

DIRECTIONS

1 Using your scissors, cut six to seven 16-inch strips of fabric from the T-shirts.

2 Hold all of the strips together and tie a knot on the end.

3 Gather the strips into three sections and braid them until you get a few inches from the end.

4 Tie another knot at the end of the braid.

5 Go find your pup and start a game of tug-of-war!

VEGGIE BREATH DOG TREATS

Your family's fur baby deserves delicious and healthy treats. These dog treats are not only a favorite, but they are all natural and will give your pooch great breath. This is perfect for you and your parents to make together in the kitchen. Simple recipes like these dog treats are a great way to help you learn your way around the kitchen and learn the fundamentals of measuring and mixing.

Age: 7+ with adult supervision

MATERIALS

- Food processor
- 2 cups gluten free old-fashioned oats
- 1 medium carrot, peeled and grated
- 1 cup fresh parsley, finely chopped
- 2 medium bowls
- 1 ripe banana peeled
- 1 large egg, beaten
- 1 tablespoon coconut oil, melted
- 1 large bowl
- Flour, for dusting
- Cookie cutter

DIRECTIONS

1 Preheat the oven to 325°F.

2 In a food processor, have an adult pulse the oats until they look consistent.

3 Combine the oats, carrots, and parsley in a bowl.

4 In a separate bowl, mash the banana and mix in the egg and coconut oil.

5 Combine banana mixture and dry ingredients in a large bowl. Mix until you get a dough consistency.

6 Dust a surface with flour and put dough on it. Use your hand to flatten the dough mixture to ¼-inch thickness.

7 Cut out the cookies using a dog bone cookie cutter.

8 Bake for 30–45 minutes or until lightly brown.

9 Remove from oven with the help of an adult. Let the treats cool on the pan for 1 hour and then give your dog a yummy treat!

ACKNOWLEDGMENTS

Our entire team would like to thank our family and friends for supporting us through our crazy crafting adventures. A special thank you to our pint-size creative models who made this book so darn cute: Olivia, Kailyn, Nicholas, Bradley, Marcella, Alexander, and Noah.

I personally would like to thank my husband, Brennan, and my parents for standing by me when I had this crazy idea to start CraftBoxGirls.com. Your support, daily encouragement and affirmations keep me going strong! I am thankful for all of our Craft Box Girls supporters, contributors, and passionate fans who have encouraged our team to push the creative limits and continue to take our creative dreams to the next level! Cheers to DIY MADE SIMPLE! #creativedreams

The making of this book was an amazing team effort and bonding experience. From brainstorming sessions to countless hours of creating crafts to long days shooting to wrangling our pint-size models, we enjoyed every second of making this magically creative book.

Everyone on our team created projects in this book. All photography was captured by Rosanna Penaflorida, Craft Box Girls COO, and Chan Vu, Craft Box Girls Director of Content.

About the Craft Box Girls

Craft Box Girls is a do-it-yourself lifestyle destination to discover how-to projects, kids crafts, simple recipes, and party tips for all ages. Discover creative projects by visiting www.CraftBoxGirls.com or downloading Craft Box Girls TV on Apple TV. Follow our creative journey by connecting with us on one of our social platforms:

facebook.com/craftboxgirls
twitter.com/craftboxgirls
instagram.com/craftboxgirls
pinterest.com/craftboxgirls
youtube.com/craftboxgirls

MEET OUR CREATIVE TEAM:

Lynn Lilly // Founder and Chief Executive Officer

Lynn's everyday life is filled with confetti, glue guns, mason jars, and sprinkles! As the founder of CraftBoxGirls.com, LifestyleBloggersSociety.com and NationalDIYDAY.com, Lynn is working to empower and inspire women and youth through creative do-it-yourself projects, crafts and simple recipes. You can catch Lynn sharing simple and easy projects on her weekly television segment on NBC's *Atlanta & Company* and as a guest on daytime television shows across the country. When Lynn is not crafting, she spends her time speaking at events and teaching crafting classes and blogging workshops. Lynn lives in Atlanta with her husband, Brennan, and their three furbabies, Lolly, Ares, and Tate. Both love kids tremendously and hope to start a family soon!

Rosanna Penaflorida // Chief Operations Officer

Rosanna not only drives the creative front for Craft Box Girls, she also plays a key role in business strategy and operations. Rosanna's creativity stems from her experience with marketing, events and business management. Her passion lies with creativity and lifestyle photography. In Atlanta, Rosanna loves long walks with her husband, Adam, and their lovable dogs, Abby and Dinny. They will soon be enjoying long walks with a new addition to the family in the summer of 2016.

Chan Vu // Director of Content

Art has always been Chan's favorite subject in school. Not only did she excel in art as a kid, she still resorts to arts and crafts as her creative outlet as an adult. It's the part of us that never has to grow up. Chan created her food, DIY and travel blog called *Sweets By Chan*, to inspire others with her creative passion. It's the sweet things in life that inspire her. From home projects to recipe hacks to crazy Craft Box Girls projects, Chan loves challenging herself to come up with creative ways to inspire others.

Allison Cawley Veyda // Editor

Allison is by far Craft Box Girls' most fashionable crafter. Allison is an integral part of the Craft Box Girls team, sharing her favorite recipes and crafts for parties and entertaining. Aside from being a part of the Craft Box Girls team, Allie runs her own lifestyle blog, *Peachfully Chic*.

Laura Carrozza // Blogger

Laura has been creating do-it-yourself content for Craft Box Girls since our inception. Laura gets her craft and sewing skills from her grandmother and currently has her own custom-made handbag line, Jersey Peach Designs.